So You Think You're IRISH

✤ ✤ ✤

margaret kelleher

WINGS BOOKS

NEW YORK

No part of this book may be reproduced or transmitted in any form or by
any means electronic or mechanical including photocopying, recording,
or by any information storage and retrieval system, without permission in
writing from the publisher.

This 1996 edition is published by Wings Books,
an imprint of Random House Value Publishing,
division of Random House, Inc., New York,
by arrangement with Historical Publishing Co.

Wings Books and colophon are trademarks of
Random House, Inc.

Random House
New York • Toronto • London • Sydney • Auckland
www.randomhouse.com

Printed and bound in the United States of America

Library of Congress Cataloging-in-Publication Data

Kelleher, Margaret.
         So you think you're Irish / Margaret Kelleher.
                p. cm.
         ISBN 0-517-05224-5
                1. Ireland—Miscellanea.   2. Irish Americans—
Miscellanea.   3. Questions and answers.
I. Title.   II. Title: So you think you are Irish.
DA906.K45   1992
941.5—dc20   91-28869
                                                     CIP

20 19 18

To my parents and sister Gemma, whose love and support travel
everywhere.

Margaret Kelleher was born in Mallow, county Cork, ancestral home of Thomas P. O'Neill, Jr. She graduated from University College Cork in 1984 with a B.A. in English and History. Currently she is working toward a doctorate in English at Boston College.

Thanks to all who donated questions and ideas: the O'Sullivan family of Templemartin, county Cork; Eleanor Byrne, Mike Dowd, Matt Jacobson, and Eoin Edwards of the *Cork Examiner*. To all my relatives and friends for their encouragement and sense of humor.

Contents

The Irish in America

"No country in the world, in the history of the world, has endured the haemorrhage which this island endured over a period of a few years for so many of its sons and daughters. These sons and daughters are scattered throughout the world and they give this small island a family of millions upon millions...in a sense, all of them who visit Ireland come home."

John F. Kennedy

1.   According to the 1980 U.S. census, how many Americans claim Irish ancestry, wholly or in part?
      a) Over ten million
      b) Over five million
      c) Over forty-three million
      d) Over three million

2.   According to the 1980 U.S. census, what percentage of this figure claims solely Irish ancestry?
      a) 10 percent
      b) 25 percent
      c) None
      d) 100 percent

3.   How many U.S. Presidents have all or part Irish ancestry?
      a) Seventeen
      b) None
      c) Ten
      d) Two

4.   How many U.S. Presidents were sons of Irish immigrants?
     a) None
     b) One
     c) Seventeen
     d) Three

5.   Whose paternal great-grandfather emigrated from county Tipperary in 1829?
     a) Ronald Reagan's
     b) Thomas P. O'Neill's
     c) Eugene O'Neill's
     d) Richard Nixon's

6.   What town in county Tipperary now boasts the Ronald Reagan Bar?
     a) Ballyporeen
     b) Clonmel
     c) Mitchelstown
     d) New Ross

7.   What U.S. President owned an Irish setter called King Timahoe, named after his ancestral home in country Laois?
     a) Andrew Jackson
     b) Richard Nixon
     c) Ulysses Grant
     d) Jimmy Carter

8.   What American President defined himself as "an Irishman by osmosis"?
     a) Gerald Ford
     b) Lyndon B. Johnson
     c) George Washington
     d) Harry S. Truman

9. According to what member of the Regan clan, those who spelt the name Reagan were common laborers?
   a) Donald Regan
   b) Nancy Reagan
   c) Patty Reagan
   d) Ronald Reagan

10. What Prime Minister and President of Ireland was born in Brooklyn, New York, in 1882?
    a) Erskine Childers
    b) Michael Collins
    c) Eamon de Valera
    d) Padraig Pearse

11. How many men of Irish ancestry signed the Declaration of Independence?
    a) None
    b) Twelve
    c) Nine
    d) Two

12. The hand of what Irish-born man wrote the Declaration of Independence?
    a) George Washington
    b) Charles Thomson
    c) Henry Adams
    d) John Dunlap

13. Who are the Scotch-Irish?
    a) Whiskey-drinking Irish
    b) Irish whiskey-drinking Scots
    c) Irish-Americans
    d) Ulster Scots

14. Who said of his fellow Scotch-Irish, "They were of all men
the best fitted to conquer the wilderness and hold it against
all-comers"?
   a) Eugene O'Neill
   b) Theodore Roosevelt
   c) Babe Ruth
   d) Ronald Reagan

15. John F. Kennedy and Ronald Reagan were the first and third
U.S. Presidents to visit Ireland while in office. Who was the
second?
   a) Jimmy Carter
   b) Richard Nixon
   c) Gerald Ford
   d) Lyndon Johnson

16. What Irish politician said of John F. Kennedy: "He was
tough, loved a laugh, and treated us as we really are. That's
why he was different, and that's why we worship the Kennedy family"?
   a) Eamon de Valera
   b) Garret Fitzgerald
   c) Sean Lemass
   d) Conor Cruise O'Brien

17. Who said of the Ulster-Irish: "They are in a fair way to taking possession of the State"?
   a) George Washington
   b) Cotton Mather
   c) Henry Adams
   d) Benjamin Franklin

18. Who said during a visit to Dublin in 1972, regarding a call by
Senator Edward Kennedy for British withdrawal from Northern Ireland, "California does not have a foreign policy"?
   a) The Beach Boys
   b) Pat Brown
   c) Ronald Reagan
   d) Jack Nicholson

19.   From what New York building is the Irish flag flown on St.
        Patrick's Day?
        a) The World Trade Center
        b) The Empire State Building
        c) City Hall
        d) Radio City Music Hall

20.   In 1886 what New York mayor attempted to end the custom?
        a) Abram S. Hewitt
        b) Al Smith
        c) Ed Kick
        d) Norman Mailer

21.   When was the St. Patrick's Day parade first held on Fifth
        Avenue?
        a) 1975
        b) 1905
        c) 1875
        d) 1805

22.   When was the earliest recorded St. Patrick's Day celebra-
        tion held in Boston?
        a) 1777
        b) 1737
        c) 1837
        d) 1877

23.   What U.S. community is unique in its celebration of a legal
        holdiay for St. Patrick's Day?
        a) Boston, Massachusetts
        b) Briarwood Beach, Ohio
        c) Butte, Montana
        d) Carmel, California

24. When was the U.S.S. Shamrock launched?
    a) St. Patrick's Day, 1863
    b) Christmas Day, 1902
    c) St. Patrick's Day, 1903
    d) January 1, 1929

25. What famous Boston-born businessman and father of three U.S. senators served as ambassador to Britain from 1937 to 1940?
    a) James Curley
    b) William Shannon
    c) Jim Kelly
    d) Joseph Patrick Kennedy

26. In 1884 what emigrant from county Antrim launched America's first newspaper syndicate service?
    a) Mark Twain
    b) Andrew Jackson
    c) Samuel McClure
    d) Bartley Hubbard

27. Who founded the *Irish World* in New York in 1870 and edited it until his death in 1913?
    a) Patrick Ford
    b) John Boyle O'Reilly
    c) John O'Hara
    d) Flann O'Brien

28. The Founder of the American Navy was born in Wexford. Who was he?
    a) John O'Leary
    b) John Barry
    c) John Paul Jones
    d) John Bull

29. What Boston clergyman graduated from Boston College in 1881 and was cardinal from 1911 until his death in 1944?
    a) Cardinal Law
    b) Cardinal O'Connell
    c) Cardinal Hughes
    d) Cardinal Cushing

30. Who in 1880 became the first Roman Catholic mayor of New York (born in county Cork in 1832)?
    a) William Russell Grace
    b) Al Smith
    c) James Michael Curley
    d) John Fitzgerald

31. What county Tyrone person has been the only member of the U.S. Senate ever to have represented three different states?
    a) James Shields
    b) Burton K. Wheeler
    c) Edward Kennedy
    d) P. T. O'Neal

32. Who declared that his favorite part of *The Last Hurrah* by Edwin O'Connor was "the part where I die"?
    a) Edwin O'Connor
    b) William Kennedy
    c) Honey Fitz Fitzgerald
    d) James Michael Curley

33. What Boston mayor had a famous daughter named Rose?
    a) John F. Fitzgerald
    b) Patrick Kennedy
    c) Andrew J. Peters
    d) Martin Lomasney

34. What Irish-American governor of New York ran for President in 1928 on the Democratic ticket?
    a) Al Smith
    b) Franklin Delano Roosevelt
    c) Adlai Stevenson
    d) Wendell Willkie

35. What member of the American Irish community was, in the later nineteenth century, a labor leader on the West Coast?
    a) James Connolly
    b) Dennis Kearney
    c) Samuel Gompers
    d) Al Smith

36. What famous boxer began studies in Boston College, left to become a plumber's apprentice and lost the job when he broke the jaw of his boss?
    a) Jack Johnson
    b) John L. Sullivan
    c) Gene Tunney
    d) Jack Dempsey

37. Who was the first Irish mayor of Boston?
    a) John Fitzgerald
    b) Hugh O'Brien
    c) Raymond Flynn
    d) James Curley

38. What Irish exile, Fenian and poet was the editor of *The Pilot* until his death in 1890?
    a) Thomas Davis
    b) John Boyle O'Reilly
    c) Geoffrey Roche
    d) John Devoy

39. What Ulsterman became the first American cardinal?
    a) Cardinal McCloskey
    b) Cardinal Law
    c) Cardinal Hughes
    d) Cardinal Cushing

40. Who declared, in an address to the New England Society of Brooklyn in 1888, "But let us have done with British-Americans and Irish-Americans and German-Americans, and so on, and all be Americans"?
    a) Henry Cabot Lodge
    b) William McKinley
    c) William Gladstone
    d) John Devoy

41. Who was elected to the U.S. Senate in 1977, having served as the U.S. ambassador to the United Nations in 1976?
    a) Daniel P. Moynihan
    b) Thomas P. O'Neill
    c) Hugh Carey
    d) Edward Kennedy

42. What holiday is celebrated in Boston on March 17?
    a) St. Patrick's Day
    b) Washington's Birthday
    c) St. Kevin's Day
    d) Evacuation Day

43. Who are the Four Horsemen of American politics?
    a) The U.S. ambassadors to Ireland, Great Britain, France and Germany
    b) The Secretaries of Defense, Education, State and the Treasury
    c) Ted Kennedy, Tip O'Neill, Hugh Carey and Daniel Moynihan
    d) The mayors of Boston, New York, Chicago and Philadelphia

44.　Who in 1981 was the first woman ever appointed to the
United States Supreme Court?
　　a) Sandra Day O'Connor
　　b) Jane Byrne
　　c) Jeanne Kirkpatrick
　　d) Dorothy Parker

45.　What Boston-born man, son of an Irish immigrant, is said
to have created the modern skyscraper?
　　a) Frank Lloyd Wright
　　b) Dennis Kearney
　　c) Louis H. Sullivan
　　d) James Michael Curley

46.　Where is the most Irish church on the continent?
　　a) San Francisco
　　b) New York
　　c) Boston
　　d) Corpus Christi, Texas

47.　Who performed the first transatlantic nonstop flight from
America to Ireland?
　　a) Amy Johnson
　　b) Charles Lindbergh
　　c) John Alcock and Arthur Brown
　　d) Amelia Earhart

48.　How many Dublins are in the United States?
　　a) Thirteen
　　b) Three
　　c) One
　　d) None

49.　Where is the town of St. Patrick?
　　a) California
　　b) Alaska
　　c) Missouri
　　d) Tennessee

50.   Where in the U.S. is the town of Londonderry?
        a) New Hampshire
        b) Ohio
        c) Vermont
        d) All of the above

51.   According to the American Kennel Club, what is the tallest breed of dog?
        a) Irish wolfhound
        b) Red setter
        c) Irish setter
        d) St. Bernard

52.   What Irish-American composer's life was celebrated in the movie *Yankee Doodle Dandy*?
        a) George M. Cohan
        b) Ned Harrigan
        c) Laurence Lerner
        d) Tim Rice

53.   What famous director was born Sean O'Feeney in Maine in 1895?
        a) John Huston
        b) George Cukor
        c) John Ford
        d) George Stevens

54.   What Dublin-born composer wrote the operetta *Babes in Toyland*?
        a) George M. Cohan
        b) Edward Harrigan
        c) Gilbert O'Sullivan
        d) Victor Herbert

55. Who was born Maureen Fitzsimmons in Dublin in 1921?
    a) Maureen O'Sullivan
    b) Maureen O'Hara
    c) Sarah Miles
    d) Yvonne deCarlo

56. Who was the daughter of Jack Kelly, the Philadelphian businessman and Olympic rower?
    a) Gene Kelly
    b) Helen Keller
    c) Grace Kelly
    d) Jackie Onassis

57. What famous Irish tenor became a U.S. citizen in 1917?
    a) James Joyce
    b) John McCormack
    c) Bartley D'Arcy
    d) Gabriel Conroy

58. What famous actor was born in Mexico in 1915 to a Mexican mother and an Irish father?
    a) John Wayne
    b) Anthony Quinn
    c) Barry Fitzgerald
    d) Dion Boucicault

59. Who wrote *Studs Lonigan*, a novel set in 1920s Chicago?
    a) Edwin O'Connor
    b) F. Scott Fitzgerald
    c) John Lonigan
    d) James T. Farrell

60. What Irish-American novelist wrote *Ironweed*?
    a) James T. Farrell
    b) John Boyle O'Reilly
    c) William Kennedy
    d) Jack Nicholson

61. The maternal grandfather of what famous writer emigrated from country Fermanagh to St. Paul, Minnesota?
    a) Garrison Keillor
    b) Ernest Hemingway
    c) Samuel Beckett
    d) F. Scott Fitzgerald

62. What novelist was born into an Irish family in Pennsylvania in 1905?
    a) Edwin O'Connor
    b) William Faulkner
    c) John O'Hara
    d) Willa Cather

63. In 1948 the Philadelphia police attempted unsuccessfully to ban what Irish-American novel?
    a) *The Great Gatsby*
    b) *The Last Hurrah*
    c) *Studs Lonigan*
    d) *Butterfield 8*

64. When did Eugene O'Neill win the Nobel Prize for literature?
    a) 1936
    b) 1926
    c) 1946
    d) 1956

65. For what novel did William Kennedy win a Pulitzer Prize in 1984?
    a) *Legs*
    b) *The Last Hurrah*
    c) *Ironweed*
    d) *All in the Family*

66. In reference to what event did John B. Yeats write from New York in 1911 to his son William: "It would be a fine fight for a fine principle"?
    a) The lifting of the ban on *Ulysses*
    b) Legislation for Irish emigrants
    c) The forthcoming tour by the Abbey Theatre
    d) Home Rule

67. What mayor of Boston sent his secretary to evaluate the Abbey's performance of *The Playboy of the Western World* in 1911, in response to objections by various Irish-American societies?
    a) Andrew J. Peters
    b) John F. Fitzgerald
    c) James Michael Curley
    d) Hugh O'Brien

68. Where, during their American tour of 1911–12, were the Abbey players assaulted with a shower of big knobbly potatoes, heavy, dusty and hard?
    a) Philadelphia
    b) New York
    c) Boston
    d) New Orleans

69. Who claimed that her fellow countrymen had identifed themselves during the New York riots by throwing what she called the national vegetable?
    a) Annie Horniman
    b) Lady Gregory
    c) Siobhan MacKenna
    d) Maureen O'Hara

70. What personal friend of Lady Gregory attended the play in support of the Abbey players?
    a) W. B. Yeats
    b) Rose Fitzgerald
    c) Theodore Roosevelt
    d) John M. Synge

71. In what American city were the Abbey players arrested and charged with the presentation of plays of an immoral nature?
    a) New York
    b) Boston
    c) Philadelphia
    d) Chicago

72. Who wrote, on hearing of the arrests and trial, ''All decent people are arrested in America. That is the reason I have refused all invitation to go there. Besides, who am I to question Philadelphia's right to make itself ridiculous''?
    a) George Bernard Shaw
    b) Oscar Wilde
    c) W. B. Yeats
    d) Lady Gregory

73. What writer named his children Shane Rudraighe and Oona?
    a) Eugene O'Neill
    b) Ezra Pound
    c) James T. Farrell
    d) F. Scott Fitzgerald

74. What Irish dramatist wrote to Eugene O'Neill, ''You write like an Irishman. You don't write like an American''?
    a) Sean O'Casey
    b) John Synge
    c) Samuel Beckett
    d) G. B. Shaw

75. What satirist created Martin Dooley, a bachelor, a saloonkeeper, and a Roscommon Irishman?
    a) Will Rogers
    b) Dorothy Parker
    c) Finley Peter Dunne
    d) Wilfrid Sheed

76. What Galway-born man composed *When Johnny Comes Marching Home?*
    a) George M. Cohan
    b) Victor Herbert
    c) Patrick Sarsfield Gilmore
    d) John Locke

77. What musical combination produced such hits as *Maggie Murphy's Home* and *Remember, Boy, You're Irish?*
    a) Lloyd and Webber
    b) Webber and Rice
    c) Rodgers and Hammerstein
    d) Harrigan and Hart

78. Who included in his credentials for his claim to be an Irishman that he was a friend of Barry Fitzgerald?
    a) John Wayne
    b) Ronald Reagan
    c) Gene Kelly
    d) Fred Astaire

79. What film version of a classic American novel, starring Gregory Peck, was filmed in Ireland?
    a) *Ryan's Daughter*
    b) *The Great Gatsby*
    c) *Moby Dick*
    d) *The Quiet Man*

80.   What native of Kilkenny designed the White House?
       a) Frank Lloyd Wright
       b) James Hoban
       c) James Kelly
       d) Louis Sullivan

81.   What Irish-American boxer held the world heavyweight title
       from 1919 to 1926?
       a) Jack Dempsey
       b) John L. Sullivan
       c) Jack Doyle
       d) Barry McGuigan

82.   Who said in New Ross, Ireland in June 1963: "Some years
       ago, an Irishman from New Ross traveled to Washington.
       In order to let his neighbors know how well he was doing,
       he had his picture taken in front of the White House. On the
       back of the picture, he wrote 'This is my summer home.
       Come and see it'"?
       a) John F. Kennedy
       b) Edward Kennedy
       c) Edwin O'Connor
       d) William Kennedy

Answers

1. c) Over forty-three million

2. b) 25 percent, i.e. over ten million

3. a) Seventeen

4. d) Three: Grant, Arthur and Jackson

5. a) Ronald Reagan's

6. a) Ballyporeen

7. b) Richard Nixon

8. b) Lyndon B. Johnson

9. d) Ronald Reagan

10. c) Eamon de Valera

11. c) Nine

12. b) Charles Thomson

13. d) Scotch-Irish is the American term for descendants of Scottish Presbyterians who settled in Ulster in the seventeenth century.

14. b) Theodore Roosevelt

15. b) Richard Nixon visited Ireland in 1971.

16. b) Garret Fitzgerald, the former prime minister of Ireland

17. d) Benjamin Franklin

18. c) Ronald Reagan

19. c) City Hall

20. a) Abram S. Hewitt

21. c) 1875, just after the new cathedral was built

22. b) 1737

23. b) Briarwood Beach, Ohio

24. a) On St. Patrick's Day, 1863, the ship was christened with Irish whiskey!

25. d) Joseph Kennedy

26. c) Samuel McClure

27.   a) Patrick Ford

28.   b) John Barry

29.   b) Cardinal O'Connell

30.   a) William Russell Grace

31.   a) In the nineteenth century James Shields was a senator for Illinois, Minnesota and Missouri.

32.   d) James Michael Curley, on whose career the book was based

33.   a) John F. "Honey Fitz" Fitzgerald

34.   a) Al Smith

35.   b) Dennis Kearney

36.   b) John L. Sullivan

37.   b) Hugh O'Brien

38.   b) John Boyle O'Reilly

39.   a) Cardinal McCloskey

40.   a) Henry Cabot Lodge

41.   a) Daniel P. Moynihan

42.   d) Evacuation Day

43.   c) Kennedy, O'Neill, Carey and Moynihan

44. a) Sandra Day O'Connor

45. c) Louis H. Sullivan

46. a) St. Patrick's Church, San Francisco

47. c) John Alcock and Arthur Brown

48. a) Thirteen

49. c) Missouri

50. d) All three states

51. a) Irish wolfhound

52. a) George M. Cohan

53. c) John Ford

54. d) Victor Herbert

55. b) Maureen O'Hara

56. c) Grace Kelly

57. b) John McCormack

58. b) Anthony Quinn

59. d) James T. Farrell

60. c) William Kennedy

61. d) F. Scott Fitzgerald

62. c) John O'Hara

63. c) *Studs Lonigan*

64. a) 1936

65. c) *Ironweed*

66. c) The forthcoming tour by the Abbey Theatre

67. b) John F. Fitzgerald

68. b) In New York, during the performance of Synge's *The Playboy of the Western World*

69. b) Lady Gregory

70. c) Former President Theodore Roosevelt

71. c) Philadelphia

72. a) George Bernard Shaw

73. a) Eugene O'Neill

74. a) Sean O'Casey

75. c) Finley Peter Dunne

76. c) Patrick Sarsfield Gilmore

77. d) Edward Harrigan and Tony Hart

78. b) Ronald Reagan, in his address to the Irish Parliament in 1984

79.   c) *Moby Dick*

80.   b) James Hoban

81.   a) Jack Dempsey

82.   a) John F. Kennedy

Beliefs, Legends, Superstitions and Remedies

"If you want to interest him [the Irishman] you've got to call the unfortunate island Kathleen ni Hoolihan and pretend she's a little old woman."

G. Bernard Shaw (*John Bull's Other Island*)

1. Who is Ireland's patron saint?
   a) St. Lawrence O'Toole
   b) St. Patrick
   c) St. Brighid
   d) Uncle Sam

2. What creature is St. Patrick said to have banished from Ireland?
   a) The lizard
   b) The snake
   c) The politician
   d) The bear

3. What Irish plant is reputed to have been used by St. Patrick to explain the doctrine of the Holy Trinity?
   a) The nettle
   b) The shamrock
   c) The thistle
   d) The cactus

plant is generally considered to be the legendary
ck?
a) Clover
b) Thistle
c) Water-cress
d) Yellow trefoil

5.   Who has the claim to fame of bringing St. Patrick to Ireland?
     a) St. Brighid
     b) Niall of the Nine Hostages
     c) Bord Failte, the Irish Tourist Board
     d) The Vikings

6.   Who will judge the Irish on Judgement Day and allow them
     into the Kingdom of Heaven?
     a) St. Peter
     b) St. Patrick
     c) Gabriel
     d) Lucifer

7.   What Irish island is named St. Patrick's Purgatory, on which
     penitents still fast for three days?
     a) Lough Derg
     b) Inismore
     c) Clare Island
     d) Tory Island

8.   To what does the following verse refer?
     "On the eighth day of March it was, some people say,/That
     Saint Patrick at midnight he first saw the day,/While others
     declare 'twas the ninth he was born. . ./Till Father Mulcahy,
     who showed them their sins,/Said 'No one could have two
     birthdays, but a twins.'/Says he, 'Boys, don't be fightin' for
     eight or for nine,/Don't be always dividin', but sometimes
     combine;/Combine eight and nine, and seventeen is the
     mark,/So let that be his birthday.' 'Amen' says the clerk.''

a) The dating of St. Patrick's Day
b) The decision by the Boston City Council to declare March 17 a holiday
c) The dating of St. Patrick's death
d) The origin of St. Patrick

9. Who is known as Mary of the Gaels?
a) Mary, mother of Christ
b) St. Brighid
c) Mary Baker Eddy
d) Mary Magdalen

10. In Celtic pre-Christian mythology, who was Brighid?
a) The goddess of healing
b) The goddess of smiths
c) The goddess of fertility and poetry
d) All of the above

11. Who was Ireland's first canonized saint?
a) St. Lawrence O'Toole
b) St. Oliver Plunkett
c) St. Matthew Talbot
d) St. Patrick

12. Who is the third patron saint of Ireland?
a) St. Cuchulainn
b) St. W. B. Yeats
c) St. Columcille
d) St. Kevin

13. Who is said to have discovered America in 545 A.D.?
a) St. Brendan, Bishop of Clonfert
b) St. Kevin
c) Irish sailors on the Spanish Armada
d) An Irish monk who sailed with the Icelander Leif Eriksson

14.   Who sailed from Dingle, county Kerry, to Boston in 1978
       to recreate the voyage?
           a) Tim Severin
           b) Ronald Reagan
           c) Brendan Grace
           d) Dennis O'Connor

15.   Who was the Celtic sun god and god of arts and crafts?
           a) Setanta
           b) Lugh
           c) Bella
           d) Jupiter

16.   What was the later name of this god of arts and crafts in Irish
       folk tradition?
           a) The pooka
           b) The weaver
           c) The leprechaun
           d) The banshee

17.   What is the leprechaun's legendary profession?
           a) Tour guide
           b) Tailor and cobbler
           c) Banker
           d) Garden ornament

18.   Whose cry heralds the death of a member of the listener's
       family?
           a) The banshee
           b) The keener
           c) The pooka
           d) A wolf

19.   What is a changeling?
           a) A unit of Irish currency
           b) Loose coins
           c) An ugly impish creature left by the fairies in place of
              a stolen child
           d) An evil spirit who-steals cattle on Halloween

20. What is a *púca* (pooka)?
    a) A mischievous, impish fairy who often takes the form
       of a horse
    b) An Irish dance
    c) A type of clothing
    d) An Irish ballad

21. What Shakespearean character represents this demon?
    a) Falstaff in *Henry IV*
    b) The ghost in *Hamlet*
    c) *Macbeth*
    d) Puck in *A Midsummer Night's Dream*

22. What weapons can be used against the fairies?
    a) None
    b) Money
    c) Fire and iron
    d) Words

23. To what Irish phenomenon was George Moore referring when
    he said, "Nothing in Ireland lasts long except the miles"?
    a) The state of Irish roads
    b) The size of Irish cars
    c) The length of an Irish mile
    d) The weather

24. What has been described as, "Four feet long, one foot wide,
    nine inches high and worth over thirty million dollars"?
    a) The Book of Kells
    b) The bar in Mulligan's pub
    c) The Cross of Cong
    d) The Blarney Stone

25. What is the name of the legendary Atlantic island that is visi-
    ble only every seven years?
    a) Southern Ireland
    b) Inismore
    c) Glengariff
    d) Hy Brasil

26.   What country was, when first discovered, believed to be this
       legendary country and named accordingly?
         a) Argentina
         b) Honduras
         c) Brazil
         d) Thailand

27.   What is believed to be the origin of fairies?
         a) The angels who revolted and were thrown out of
         heaven
         b) The ancient gods driven underground by
         Christianity
         c) Products of the imagination
         d) Products of international marketing

28.   What is "blarney"?
         a) Lies
         b) Flattery so thin we like it
         c) Gaelic
         d) Insults

29.   When was Blarney Castle built?
         a) 1546
         b) 1446
         c) 1846
         d) 446

30.   What does kissing the Blarney Stone reputedly bestow?
         a) Good luck
         b) Fertility
         c) The gift of the gab
         d) Rheumatism

31.   What are the reputed origins of the Blarney Stone?
         a) It is Jacob's Pillow brought back from the Holy Land
            after the Crusades.

b) An invention of the Irish Tourist Board
c) An incentive to tourists to come to an area where woollens and crystal are sold
d) Part of the Wailing Wall of Jerusalem

32. Who is credited with first using the word "blarney"?
a) Cormac of Munster
b) Dion Boucicault
c) Queen Elizabeth the First
d) Queen Victoria

33. In what river was it said that Irish people should be dipped in order to lose bashfulness or inhibition?
a) The Shannon
b) The Liffey
c) The Lee
d) The Nile

34. Who is the legendary Irish hero, whose name originated in his boyhood murder of a hound?
a) Cuchulainn
b) Oisin
c) Patrick
d) Kevin

35. Which of the following did not invade Ireland?
a) The Vikings
b) The Romans
c) The Normans
d) The English

36. The Fomorii are the evil gods of Irish myth. Where was their center?
a) Tara
b) Dublin
c) Tory Island
d) Cork

37. In Irish legend, which of the following three goddesses won her appeal to have her name accepted as the name of the country?
    a) Banba
    b) Eire
    c) Fodla

38. In Irish myth, what animal had sacred qualities?
    a) The boar
    b) The bull
    c) The stag
    d) All of the above

39. Where was the seat of the High Kings of Ireland?
    a) Tara
    b) Dublin Castle
    c) Armagh
    d) Galway

40. In Irish legend, Spain is a synonym for what region?
    a) The Land of Promise
    b) The Land of Death
    c) The Eternal Region
    d) The Remotest Region

41. Who were the Red Branch warriors?
    a) The legendary quardians of Ulster
    b) The Fenians
    c) The men of 1916
    d) The supporters of King James II

42. The Irish word for parliament, *Dáil*, derives from the word for what?
    a) A conversation
    b) A tribe or land inhabited by a tribe
    c) An election
    d) Blindness

43.   The term Fenian derives from the name of what legendary
      band of warriors?
      a) The Fianna
      b) The Red Branch
      c) The Incas
      d) The men of 1848

44.   Which of the following is not a mythical representation of
      Ireland?
      a) A beautiful maiden in a dream
      b) An old woman
      c) A black rose
      d) An armor-clad warrior

45.   In Irish legend and history, how many provinces were there?
      a) Four
      b) Five
      c) Three
      d) None

46.   According to the Irish saying, what should one do at a wake?
      a) Sing a song
      b) Cry
      c) Drink alcohol
      d) Play games

47.   What are Dividing the Meat, Selling the Pig and Catching
      the Herrings?
      a) Activities not to be performed on Sundays
      b) Traditional games played at Irish wakes
      c) Traditional summer employment
      d) Sources of income

48.   Who are described in the following way?

            They live upon the dead,
            By letting out their persons by the hours
            To mimic sorrow when the heart's not sad.

Professional actors

Professional keeners, hired to lament the dead

) Priests

d) Banshees

49.   The Irish provinces today are Munster, Ulster, Leinster and
       Connaught. What was the fifth province in Irish legend?
       a) Galway
       b) England
       c) Meath
       d) Tyrone

50.   What, according to Irish tradition, should be placed next
       to a corpse?
       a) A piece of a candle
       b) A coin
       c) A small quantity of wine or spirits
       d) All of the above

51.   If, on a journey, you meet a red-haired woman, what should
       you do?
       a) Turn back
       b) Talk to her
       c) Ignore her
       d) Cross the road

52.   If you meet a funeral on the road, what should you do?
       a) Stop
       b) Take three steps backwards
       c) Keep walking
       d) Turn back

53.   Which of the following was traditionally believed to be pro-
       tection against bad luck?
       a) A four-leafed shamrock

b) Holy water

c) Goose-grease

d) Salt

e) All of the above

54. On New Year's Eve, what should you receive from a black-haired stranger?

a) A coin

b) A piece of cake

c) A piece of coal

d) A piece of soap

55. The belief that evil-doers could place charms and thus destroy or steal dairy produce is called what?

a) *Ciotóg*

b) Shebeen

c) *Piseog*

d) Brogue

56. What were considered the best days for gathering medicinal herbs?

a) May Eve and May Day

b) The first days of the year

c) The last days of the year

d) Christmas week

57. Which of the following strategies enabled a spell to be placed, thus causing the victim's crop to fail?

a) Uttering a charm while watching the smoke rising from the victim's chimney

b) Opening every gate and door on the victim's farm

c) Tapping the victim's animals with a hazel switch

d) Burying meat or eggs in the neighbor's fields

e) All of the above

58.   Why should the face be anointed with the blood of a bull or of a hare?
       a) To get rid of freckles
       b) As a facial cleanser
       c) As a moisturizer
       d) For good health

59.   What is a country traditional cure for chest colds and coughs?
       a) Sour milk
       b) Carrageen moss (edible seaweed) simmered in water and lemon juice
       c) Goose-grease
       d) Pig fat

60.   What should be rubbed into chapped hands to cure them?
       a) Soap
       b) Candlewick
       c) Melted mutton fat
       d) Goose-grease

61.   What is said to relieve sore throats?
       a) Alcohol
       b) Blessed water
       c) Eating grass
       d) Chewing a clove of garlic

62.   What plant was used as a cure for kidney infections?
       a) The shamrock
       b) The dandelion
       c) The nettle
       d) Garlic

63.   What gets rid of the smell of garlic from one's breath?
       a) Eating fresh parsley
       b) Nothing

      c) Drinking water
      d) Eating an onion

64.   What was said to prevent varicose veins?
      a) Molasses melted in warm water, taken every
      morning
      b) Walking
      c) Onions
      d) Red meat

65.   What was given to people with upset stomachs?
      a) Whipped egg whites with sugar added
      b) Water
      c) Whiskey
      d) Mashed potatoes

66.   What flower was used as a nerve tonic?
      a) Dandelions
      b) Thistles
      c) Cowslip blossoms
      d) Nettles

67.   What are pampooties?
      a) Irish dances
      b) An Irish dish
      c) Traditional gloves
      d) Traditional footwear, made of untanned leather

68.   What is a *crios*?
      a) A belt or girdle worn in early Christian Ireland
      b) A musical instrument played by Irish bands
      c) Traditional footwear
      d) A type of ballad

69.   What is a *léine*?
      a) A traditional tool

b) A traditional linen tunic
c) A type of house
d) A type of food

70.   What saint was made welcome on the night of January 31
       in Irish households by placing food on the windowsill or
       rushes on the threshold?
       a) St. Patrick
       b) St. Brighid
       c) St. Mary
       d) St. Francis

71.   According to tradition, what day should nobody be without
       meat?
       a) Easter Saturday
       b) Shrove Tuesday
       c) Ash Wednesday
       d) Good Friday

72.   What animal, especially if licked on Shrove Tuesday, was
       traditionally believed to endow the tongue with a cure for
       burns and scalds?
       a) A cow
       b) A rabbit
       c) A lizard
       d) A horse

73.   Under Church law until the early twentieth century, when
       was it forbidden to marry?
       a) During Lent
       b) Never
       c) After 12:00 noon
       d) On Sunday

74.   What was the most favored day for marrying in rural Ireland?
       a) Christmas Day

b) Good Friday
c) Ash Wednesday
d) Shrove Tuesday

75. What day was traditionally known as Chalk Sunday?
a) The first Sunday in Lent
b) The last Sunday of the year
c) The first Sunday of the year
d) Every Sunday

76. What days are still black fast days in Ireland, when no meat and only one main meal may be eaten?
a) Ash Wednesday and Good Friday
b) Every Friday
c) The first Friday of every month
d) The day after Christmas

77. On what day during Lent were all restrictions set aside?
a) St. Patrick's Day
b) One day, as chosen by the fasting person
c) Never
d) Every third day

78. On St. Patrick's Day, what do people in Ireland wear?
a) Green clothing
b) A shamrock
c) Red, white and blue flags
d) Orange sashes

79. What kind of weather was welcomed on Good Friday?
a) Cold and wet
b) Sunny
c) A solar eclipse
d) Snow

80.　According to tradition, a boy born on what day was destined for high office in the Church?
　　　a) St. Patrick's Day
　　　b) Easter Sunday
　　　c) June 21, the longest day of the year
　　　d) December 21, the shortest day of the year

81.　What plant was considered unlucky and not to be brcught into the house?
　　　a) The shamrock
　　　b) The palm
　　　c) The whitethorn
　　　d) Garlic

82.　At what time of year was abduction by the fairies most to be feared?
　　　a) The month of May
　　　b) Christmas
　　　c) Easter
　　　d) During snowy weather

83.　What days in Ireland are called the "Borrowed Days" and are traditionally associated with bad weather?
　　　a) The first three days in April
　　　b) The last three days of the year
　　　c) St. Patrick's Day and the day following
　　　d) Christmas vacation

84.　On what day was it believed no one should set out on a journey?
　　　a) A cold day
　　　b) A foggy day
　　　c) Whit Sunday
　　　d) Christmas Eve

Answers

1.   b) St. Patrick

2.   b) The snake

3.   b) The shamrock, the Irish national symbol since the seventeenth century

4.   d) The yellow trefoil, a plant with three leaves and one stem

5.   b) Niall of the Nine Hostages

6.   b) The impartial St. Patrick

7.   a) Lough Derg

8.   a) The dating of St. Patrick's Day

9. b) St. Brighid, the second patron saint of Ireland

10. d) Brighid, later Christianized as St. Brighid, was the goddess of healing, smiths, fertility and poetry.

11. a) St. Lawrence O'Toole

12. c) St. Columcille

13. a) St. Brendan

14. a) Tim Severin

15. b) *Lugh*

16. c) The leprechaun, from the Gaelic *lugh chromain* or little stooping Lugh, in reference to the believed driving of the old gods underground

17. b) Tailor and cobbler, but if handled correctly, he may lead you to a pot of gold

18. a) The banshee, literally *bean sidhe* or woman of the fairies

19. c) A creature left by the fairies

20. a) An impish fairy

21. d) Puck

22. c) Fire and iron

23. c) The inordinate length of the Irish mile

24. d) The Blarney Stone

25.　　d)　Hy Brasil

26.　　c)　Brazil

27.　　b)　The ancient gods driven underground by Christianity

28.　　b)　As defined by Bishop Fulton J. Sheen, who distinguished blarney from baloney, the latter being flattery so thick it cannot be true

29.　　b)　1446

30.　　c)　The gift of the gab

31.　　a)　Legend has it the stone is Jacob's Pillow.

32.　　c)　Queen Elizabeth the First, who described the efforts by the Lord of Blarney to avoid renouncing the Irish traditional system of election and the taking of tenure of his lands from the Crown as, ''This is all Blarney. What he says he never means.''

33.　　a)　The Shannon

34.　　a)　Cuchulainn, literally, the hound of Culann

35.　　b)　The Romans, who stopped at Britain

36.　　c)　Tory Island

37.　　b)　Eire

38.　　d)　The boar, bull and stag

39.　　a)　Tara

40. b) The Land of Death

41. a) The legendary guardians of Ulster

42. b) A tribe

43. a) The Fianna

44. d) An armor-clad warrior

45. b) Five: the Irish word for province is *cúige* or fifth.

46. a) Sing a song at a wake, and shed a tear when a child is born.

47. b) Traditional games played at wakes

48. b) Keeners

49. c) Meath, meaning middle, was located in the center of the country.

50. d) The candle was to give the deceased light; the money to pay his fare over the river of death; and liquor to sustain him on his journey.

51. a) Turn back

52. b) Take three steps backward

53. e) All of the above

54. c) A piece of coal

55. c) *Piseog*

56.   a) May Eve and May Day

57.   e) All of the above

58.   a) To get rid of freckles

59.   b) Carrageen moss

60.   c) Melted mutton fat

61.   d) Chewing garlic

62.   b) The dandelion

63.   a) Eating fresh parsley

64.   a) Molasses

65.   a) Egg whites

66.   c) Cowslip blossoms

67.   d) This footwear has survived in the Aran Islands into modern times.

68.   a) A belt or girdle

69.   b) A traditional linen tunic

70.   b) St. Brighid. It was generally believed that the saint traveled about the countryside on the night before her festival, blessing people and livestock.

71.   b) Shrove Tuesday

72.   c) A lizard

73.   a) During Lent

74.   d) Shrove Tuesday

75.   a) The first Sunday in Lent, because those who remained
           unmarried had their clothes decorated with chalk

76.   a) Ash Wednesday and Good Friday

77.   a) St. Patrick's Day

78.   b) A sprig of shamrock, worn on the lapel of your coat

79.   a) Cold and wet weather was interpreted as a sign of
           nature's mourning for the death of Christ.

80.   b) Easter Sunday

81.   c) The whitethorn

82.   a) May

83.   a) The first three days in April

84.   c) Whit Sunday, the first Sunday in June

History

"Politics is the chloroform of the Irish people, or rather the hashish."

Oliver St. John Gogarty

1. When are the earliest settlers reputed to have arrived in Ireland?
    a) 600 A.D.
    b) 200 A.D.
    c) 2000 B.C.
    d) 6000 B.C.

2. When is it estimated that the Celts reached Ireland?
    a) 200 A.D.
    b) 4000 B.C.
    c) 500 B.C.
    d) 500 A.D.

3. The Giant's Causeway in county Antrim consists of 37,000 columns formed by cooling lava how many years ago?
    a) Sixty million
    b) Two million
    c) One million
    d) Six thousand

4.   From when does the megalithic passage-grave at Newgrange, county Meath, date?
       a) 2500 B.C.
       b) 500 B.C.
       c) 1000 B.C.
       d) 500 A.D.

5.   The following are legendary rulers of Ireland. Rank them in historical order, beginning with those believed to be the earliest inhabitants.
       a) Tuatha De Danann
       b) Milesians
       c) Firbolg

6.   When was Ireland converted to Christianity?
       a) The third century
       b) The fifth century
       c) The twelfth century
       d) The tenth century

7.   When did Viking attacks on Ireland begin?
       a) 800 A.D.
       b) 600 A.D
       c) 1200 A.D
       d) 500 A.D.

8.   What do the following have in common: sterility, blabbing about the marriage bed, being a churchman, failure of maintenance?
       a) Ancient Irish curses
       b) Reasons for which a woman could divorce her husband in early Irish law
       c) Legal grounds for separation in contemporary Ireland
       d) Offenses punishable by death in early Ireland

9. The Battle of Clontarf in 1014 marked the decisive defeat
of the Vikings. Who led the Irish side?
   a) Strongbow
   b) Robert Bruce
   c) Brian Boru
   d) St. Patrick

10. Of whom was it traditionally said that they became more
Irish than the Irish themselves?
   a) The Spanish Armada
   b) American tourists
   c) English tourists
   d) The Norman settlers in Ireland

11. What was Sir Walter Raleigh reputed to have planted in
Youghal, county Cork, in 1585?
   a) Tobacco
   b) Potatoes
   c) Peanuts
   d) Leeks

12. In 1695 much of the Irish Army fled to Europe. These
military men became known as what?
   a) The Wild Geese
   b) The Stalwart Few
   c) Mercenaries
   d) The Lost Exiles

13. Who, in the middle of the seventeenth century, offered the
Catholic Irish the choice of going to hell or to Connaught?
   a) James Stuart
   b) Oliver Cromwell
   c) Henry VIII
   d) The O'Neill clan

14.   When was the Battle of the Boyne, between the Catholic supporters of James II and the Protestant supporters of William of Orange?

        a) 1601
        b) 1690
        c) 1740
        d) 1860

15.   Of what part of Ireland did Oliver Cromwell say that it had ''no timber to hang a man, no water to drown a man, nor no earth to bury a man''?

        a) Connemara
        b) The Burren
        c) Kerry
        d) All of Ireland

16.   What do the following nationalist patriots have in common: Wolfe Tone, Charles Stewart Parnell, Robert Emmet and Roger Casement?

        a) They were all Protestant.
        b) They were all born in Dublin.
        c) They served in the British Parliament.
        d) They all spoke French.

17.   Who said: ''When my country takes her place among the nations of the earth, then, and not till then, let my epitaph be written''?

        a) Charles Stewart Parnell
        b) Robert Emmet
        c) Padraig Pearse
        d) James Connolly

18.   When did Irish Catholics receive the right to enter Parliament without taking the Oath of Supremacy to the English crown?

        a) 1899

b) Never
c) 1829
d) 1921

19. Who is reputed to have donated 2,000 pounds in aid of Irish Relief during the potato famine of the 1840s?
   a) Ulysses S. Grant
   b) Queen Victoria
   c) The Pope
   d) James Polk

20. Who in 1830 was the first Catholic to enter the House of Commons?
   a) Daniel O'Connell
   b) Robert Emmet
   c) Charles Stewart Parnell
   d) Padraig Pearse

21. Where did the potato blight of the 1840s, which led to famine in Ireland, originate?
   a) Ireland
   b) England
   c) Turkey
   d) The United States

22. In 1841 the area comprising the present Republic of Ireland had a population of what?
   a) 3.5 million
   b) 4.5 million
   c) 5.5 million
   d) 6.5 million

23. Due to the potato famines of 1846 and 1847, with resulting deaths and large-scale emigration, by 1851 the same area had a population of what?
   a) 5.1 million

b) 2.2 million
c) 3.1 million
d) 6.1 million

24. In 1835 the number of Irish speakers was estimated at four million. The decimation of the largely Irish-speaking rural class reduced the number of Irish speakers by 1891 to what?
   a) 680,000
   b) One million
   c) 2.5 million
   d) Three million

25. The regions in Ireland where Irish is still spoken as the first language of the community are known as what?
   a) *Gaeltachts*
   b) The Pale
   c) *Fáinnes*
   d) There are no such communities.

26. What organization also known as the Fenians was founded in 1858?
   a) The United Irishmen
   b) The Young Irelanders
   c) The Irish Republican Brotherhood
   d) Sinn Fein

27. In 1866 what country did the Fenians attempt to invade and then exchange for Ireland?
   a) Canada
   b) Bermuda
   c) England
   d) Scotland

28. Who was known as the Uncrowned King of Ireland?
   a) Charles Stewart Parnell
   b) Daniel O'Connell

c) Eamon de Valera

d) Michael Collins

29.   In whose divorce case was Charles Stewart Parnell named in 1890, thus causing a split in his party?
a) Katherine O'Shea's
b) Maud Gonne's
c) Kathleen ni Houlihan's
d) Constance Markievicz's

30.   Who founded the Irish Socialist Revolutionary Party in 1896 declaring, "The great appear great because we are on our knees: let us arise"?
a) James Connolly
b) Padraig Pearse
c) James Plunkett
d) Sean O'Casey

31.   At the graveside of O'Donovan Rossa in 1915, who said, "The fools, the fools, the fools, they have left us our Fenian dead, and while Ireland holds these graves Ireland unfree shall never be at peace"?
a) Padraig Pearse
b) W. B. Yeats
c) Douglas Hyde
d) Ross O'Donovan

32.   Who declared on Easter Monday, April 24, 1916, "We are going out to be slaughtered"?
a) John McBride
b) Eamon de Valera
c) James Connolly
d) Padraig Pearse

33. How many men were executed after the Easter Rising, 1916?
    a) None
    b) Fifteen
    c) Two
    d) Ten

34. Who declared that these executions would canonize their heroes?
    a) Woodrow Wilson
    b) Lloyd George
    c) George Bernard Shaw
    d) King George V

35. What famous work begins, ''Soldiers are we, whose lives are pledged to Ireland''?
    a) The Irish Constitution
    b) The Proclamation of Independence
    c) The Irish National Anthem
    d) The Irish Constitution, revised edition

36. Of whom did George Bernard Shaw write in 1916, ''His real offence is not merely that of being an Irishman but of being a nationalist Irishman''?
    a) Padraig Pearse
    b) Wolfe Tone
    c) Sir Roger Casement
    d) Robert Emmet

37. What was the first country to recognize Ireland's independence?
    a) England
    b) France
    c) The United States
    d) Australia

38. How many Irishmen volunteered for the British forces between 1914 and 1918?
    a) None
    b) 300,000
    c) 15,000
    d) 150,000

39. Who returned to Ireland from his American fund-raising tour in 1920, via Liverpool, by hiding in a container filled with potatoes?
    a) Eamon de Valera
    b) Michael Collins
    c) Liam Cosgrave
    d) Roger Casement

40. The Treaty of December 1921 marked the beginning of what episode in Irish history?
    a) The Easter Rising
    b) The War of Independence
    c) The Civil War
    d) The Penal Laws

41. Who was the first woman to be elected to the House of Commons?
    a) Countess Markievicz
    b) Bernadette Devlin
    c) Lady Astor
    d) Margaret Thatcher

42. When did Irishwomen receive the right to vote?
    a) 1929
    b) 1919
    c) 1939
    d) 1925

43. In 1943 who declared his ideal vision of Ireland as "a land whose countryside would be bright with cosy homesteads, whose fields and villages would be joyous with the sounds of industry, with the romping of sturdy children, the contest of athletic youths, and the laughter of comely maidens"?
    a) Eamon de Valera
    b) W. B. Yeats
    c) John P. Kennedy
    d) Padraig Pearse

44. In 1969 who became the youngest woman ever elected to the British House of Commons?
    a) Margaret Thatcher
    b) Shirley Williams
    c) Mairead Williams
    d) Bernadette Devlin

45. Who said, in 1934, on the question of emigration, "No longer shall our children, like our cattle, be brought up for export"?
    a) Charles Haughey
    b) Sean MacBride
    c) Eamon de Valera
    d) Sean Lemass

46. What Nazi sympathizer was born in New York and educated at the Jesuit School in Galway?
    a) William Joyce
    b) Benito Mussolini
    c) Lord Haw-Haw
    d) Eamon de Valera

47. On which side did Ireland fight during World War II?
    a) The Allies
    b) The Axis powers

c) None

d) Japan

48. In 1940 whom did the U.S. ambassador in Dublin describe as probably the most adroit politician in Europe?
    a) Winston Churchill
    b) Eamon de Valera
    c) Adolf Hitler
    d) Charles de Gaulle

49. Who said in an address to the Irish Parliament in June 1963, "Ireland is moving in the mainstream of current world events. . .Your future is as promising as your past is proud and your destiny lies not as a peaceful island in a sea of trouble but as a maker and a shaper of world peace"?
    a) John F. Kennedy
    b) Eamon de Valera
    c) Queen Elizabeth I
    d) Pope John XXIII

50. Who declared in 1941, "Eire's neutrality must be respected. A neutral Irish Free State is of greater value to us than a hostile Ireland"?
    a) Benito Mussolini
    b) Charles de Gaulle
    c) Adolf Hilter
    d) Winston Churchill

51. In 1940 who declared on the question of Irish neutrality that "the Irish must realize that in the end they will have to fish or cut bait"?
    a) Joseph P. Kennedy
    b) John Foster Dulles
    c) Franklin D. Roosevelt
    d) Neville Chamberlain

52. Who said in 1944, "I tried hard before the United States entered the war to get de Valera to abandon neutrality and join in. I told him he would not get away with it . . . but de Valera did get away with it . . . Howbeit, that powerless little cabbage garden called Ireland wins in the teeth of all the mighty powers. *Erin go bragh*"?
    a) W. B. Yeats
    b) George Bernard Shaw
    c) Conor Cruise O'Brien
    d) Sean MacBride

53. In response to whose criticism of Irish neutrality during World War II did Eamon de Valera declare Ireland to be a "small nation that could never be got to accept defeat and has never surrendered her soul"?
    a) Franklin D. Roosevelt
    b) Winston Churchill
    c) Adolf Hitler
    d) Elizabeth II

54. When was Stormont, the Northern Irish Parliament, replaced by direct rule from Westminister?
    a) 1922
    b) 1982
    c) 1972
    d) 1962

55. When was Northern Ireland established as a political entity?
    a) 1920
    b) 1969
    c) 1890
    d) 1900

56. When was Bloody Sunday?
    a) January 30, 1972
    b) January 30, 1982

      c) January 30, 1969

      d) January 30, 1979

57.   Who was the first Irish President to die in office?
      a) Douglas Hyde
      b) Eamon de Valera
      c) John F. Kennedy
      d) Erskine Childers

58.   Who said in 1981, "If I die, God will understand"?
      a) Francis Hughes
      b) Bobby Sands
      c) Bernadette Devlin
      d) Terence McSwiney

59.   Of whom did Conor Cruise O'Brien say, "If I saw [him] buried at midnight at a crossroads, with a stake driven through his heart—politically speaking—I should continue to wear a clove of garlic round my neck, just in case"?
      a) Charles Haughey
      b) Garret Fitzgerald
      c) Desmond O'Malley
      d) Harold Wilson

60.   At whose grave in Bodenstown is an annual commemoration still held?
      a) Theobald Wolfe Tone's
      b) Robert Emmet's
      c) James Joyce's
      d) Oliver Cromwell's

Answers

1. d) 6000 B.C., in the Mesolithic period or Middle Stone Age

2. c) The Celts probably arrived in the sixth century before Christ and soon came to dominate earlier settlers.

3. a) Sixty million

4. a) Around 2500 B.C.

5. c), a), b)

6. b) The fifth century

7. a) 800 A.D.

8. b) Reasons for which a woman could divorce her husband, some of which applied until the twelfth century

History—Answers

9.   c) Brian Boru

10. d) The Normans

11. b) Potatoes

12. a) The Wild Geese

13. b) Oliver Cromwell

14. b) 1690

15. b) The Burren

16. a) They were all Protestant.

17. b) Emmet, in his famous speech from the dock, 1803

18. c) 1829, in an event known as Catholic Emancipation

19. b) Queen Victoria, who still managed to become known as "The Famine Queen"

20. a) Daniel O'Connell, "The Liberator"

21. d) The U.S.

22. d) 6.5 million—present-day population is 3.5 million.

23. a) 5.1 million, a decline of 1.4 million in ten years

24. a) 680,000

25. a) *Gaeltachts*

26. c) The Irish Republican Brotherhood

27.   a) Fenians in the U.S. attempted to invade Canada.

28.   a) Parnell

29.   a) Katherine, Kitty O'Shea

30.   a) James Connolly

31.   a) Padraig Pearse

32.   c) James Connolly

33.   b) Fifteen

34.   c) G. B. Shaw

35.   c) The Irish National Anthem

36.   c) Sir Roger Casement

37.   c) The U.S.

38.   b) 300,000

39.   a) Eamon de Valera

40.   c) The Civil War

41.   a) Countess Markievicz, in 1919, although as a member of Sinn Fein she did not take the seat

42.   b) 1919 (American women received the right in 1920.)

43.   a) Eamon de Valera

44.   d) Bernadette Devlin

45.   c) Eamon de Valera

46.   Both a) and c) Lord Haw-Haw was the nickname of William Joyce, who broadcast for Hitler with a mock British accent.

47.   c) Ireland was officially neutral during World War II.

48.   b) Eamon de Valera

49.   a) John F. Kennedy

50.   c) Hitler

51.   c) President Franklin D. Roosevelt

52.   b) G. B. Shaw

53.   b) Winston Churchill

54.   c) 1972

55.   a) 1920

56.   a) January 30, 1972

57.   d) Erskine Childers

58.   b) Bobby Sands

59.   a) Charles Haughey

60.   a) Wolfe Tone's

Arts and Entertainment

"God made the grass, the air and the rain; and the grass, the air and the rain made the Irish; and the Irish turned the grass, the air and the rain back into God."

Sean O'Faolain

1. What famous work of fiction ends: "His soul swooned slowly as he heard the snow falling faintly through the universe and faintly falling, like the descent of their last end, upon all the living and the dead"?
   a) *The Lonely Passion of Judith Hearne*
   b) "The Dead"
   c) "Guests of the Nation"
   d) *Finnegans Wake*

2. Who wrote, "I could not write the words Mr. Joyce uses: my prudish hands would refuse to form the letters?"
   a) W. B. Yeats
   b) George Bernard Shaw
   c) Ernest Hemingway
   d) Gertrude Stein

3. In 1907 who sent a telegram to W. B. Yeats in Scotland saying, "Audience broke up in disorder at word 'shift.' What

should I do?''
   a) John M. Synge
   b) Barry Fitzgerald
   c) Maud Gonne
   d) Lady Gregory

4.   What play contained this controversial word ''shift'' (meaning woman's undergarment)?
   a) *The Playboy of the Western World*
   b) *The Death of Cuchulain*
   c) *Riders to the Sea*
   d) *Juno and the Paycock*

5.   At the performance of what Abbey Theatre play in 1926 did W. B. Yeats declare to the rioting audience, ''You have disgraced yourselves again''?
   a) *The Plough and the Stars*
   b) *The Silver Tassie*
   c) *Riders to the Sea*
   d) *The Iceman Cometh*

6.   What Irish writer left Ireland for London after the banning of the book *The Dark* in 1965?
   a) James Joyce
   b) Edna O'Brien
   c) Samuel Beckett
   d) John McGahern

7.   What do the following authors have in common: J. D. Salinger, Ernest Hemingway, William Faulkner, James Joyce and Theodore Dreiser?
   a) They all had Irish ancestors.
   b) Each had work(s) banned by the Irish Censorship Board.
   c) Each lived for a time in Dublin.
   d) Each had an Irish-born wife.

8. Who defined himself as the Brother, the plain people of Ireland, Sir Myles na gCopaleen, the man who spoke Irish at a time when it was neither profitable nor popular?
    a) Brian O'Nolan
    b) Jonathan Swift
    c) Flann O'Brien
    d) Oscar Wilde

9. Whose "Modest Proposal" suggested the eating of young children as a solution to Ireland's economic problem?
    a) Edmund Burke's
    b) Rudyard Kipling's
    c) William Gladstone's
    d) Jonathan Swift's

10. Whose "Elegy on the Death of a Mad Dog" ends its account of reciprocated bites with the words, "The man recovered of the bite/The dog it was that died"?
    a) Thomas Gray
    b) James Clarence Mangan
    c) Oliver Goldsmith
    d) Thomas Moore

11. In what O'Casey play does a character exclaim, "Sacred Heart of the Crucified Jesus, take away our hearts o' stone...and give us hearts o' flesh"?
    a) *Riders to the Sea*
    b) *Juno and the Paycock*
    c) *The Plough and the Stars*
    d) *Translations*

12. Sean O'Casey's play *The Plough and the Stars* is set in what year?
    a) 1922
    b) 1866
    c) 1916
    d) 1798

13. Who wrote a play, the length of which is equal to the inhaling and exhaling of a single breath?
    a) Brian Friel
    b) Graham Reid
    c) Samuel Beckett
    d) James Joyce

14. How many Irishmen have won the Nobel Prize for literature?
    a) None
    b) One
    c) Two
    d) Three

15. Name them.

16. What Beckett character ordered his body, mind and soul to be burnt and placed in a paper bag and brought to the Abbey Theatre, that the chain be there pulled upon them, if possible during the performance of a piece?
    a) Molloy
    b) Murphy
    c) Godot
    d) Vladimir

17. What musical piece was premiered in Fishamble Street in Dublin on April 13, 1742?
    a) *Yankee Doodle Dandy*
    b) *Finian's Rainbow*
    c) *The Messiah*
    d) *Handel's Water Music*

18. What is Bono's real name?
    a) Bob Geldof
    b) Adam Hewison
    c) Johnny Fingers
    d) Larry Mullins

19. Who wrote the Irish National Anthem, "A Soldier's Song"?
     a) Brendan Behan
     b) Peadar Kearney
     c) George M. Cohan
     d) W. B. Yeats

20. What famous Irish singer was created a Papal Count in 1928?
     a) Josef Locke
     b) James Joyce
     c) Frank Patterson
     d) John McCormack

21. Who wrote the song "Four Green Fields"?
     a) Thomas Davis
     b) Tommy Makem
     c) Bob Geldof
     d) Peadar Kearney

22. What are *Ag Baint an Fhéir* (The Haymaker's Jig) and *Staicín na nEorna* (Stacks of Barley)?
     a) Traditional recipes
     b) Traditional Irish dances
     c) Activities not permitted on Sunday
     d) The official songs of county Mayo

23. From what Synge play is the following extract taken: "They're all gone now, and there isn't anything more the sea can do to me"?
     a) *Riders to the Sea*
     b) *The Playboy of the Western World*
     c) *Da*
     d) *Translations*

24. When was the Irish Literary Theatre founded (later to become the Abbey Theatre)?
     a) 1698

b) 1898
c) 1908
d) 1901

25. Who described the cracked lookingglass of a servant as a symbol of Irish art?
   a) Oscar Wilde
   b) Paul Henry
   c) James Joyce
   d) Stephen Dedalus

26. Who directed the 1987 movie based on "The Dead"?
   a) Donal McCann
   b) John Ford
   c) John Huston
   d) Merchant Ivory

27. What novel begins: "Stately plump Buck Mulligan came from the stairhead, bearing a bowl of lather on which a mirror and a razor lay crossed"?
   a) *Trinity*
   b) *Ulysses*
   c) *Finnegans Wake*
   d) *Murphy*

28. Who wrote the novel *Trinity*?
   a) Leon Uris
   b) Thomas Flanagan
   c) John McGahern
   d) William Kennedy

29. From what poem is the following refrain: "All changed, changed utterly:/A terrible beauty is born"?
   a) "Easter 1916"
   b) "September 1913"
   c) "The National Anthem"
   d) "Danny Boy"

30.   Who wrote a cycle of plays based on the life and death of
        Cuchulainn?
        a) Lady Gregory
        b) Eugene O'Neill
        c) Padraig Pearse
        d) W. B. Yeats

31.   Finish the verse: "O Ireland, isn't it grand you look like a
        bride in her rich adorning, with all the pent-up love in my
        heart I wish you _____."
        a) An exile's yearning
        b) The top of the morning
        c) *Erin go bragh*
        d) The weather's turning

32.   What famous Irish actress died in 1987?
        a) Maureen O'Hara
        b) Grace Kelly
        c) Siobhan McKenna
        d) Maud Gonne

33.   To whom did W. B. Yeats dedicate much of his love poetry?
        a) Kathleen ni Houlihan
        b) Sarah Yeats
        c) Dark Rosaleen
        d) Maud Gonne

34.   What famous manuscript is housed in the Long Room, in
        Trinity College Library in Dublin?
        a) The Magna Carta
        b) The Book of Kells
        c) The Lindisfarne Gospels
        d) The Declaration of Independence

35.   Whose mother, under the penname Speranza, contributed
        patriotic ballads to *The Nation* in the nineteenth century?

71

a) Oscar Wilde's
b) W. B. Yeats's
c) George Bernard Shaw's
d) Padraig Pearse's

36. What famous Old Irish epic centers on a married couple's rivalry over cattle?
a) *The Death of Cuchulainn*
b) *The Midnight Court*
c) *The Red Bull*
d) *The Cattle Raid of Cooley*

37. Of what Irish poet did W. H. Auden say, "Mad Ireland hurt you into poetry"?
a) W. B. Yeats
b) Oliver Goldsmith
c) Seamus Heaney
d) Jonathan Swift

38. What is a *bodhran* [bow-rawn]?
a) A musical instrument
b) A type of cow
c) A farm-tool
d) A musical tune

39. What Irish rock group included Phil Lynott as lead singer?
a) Thin Lizzy
b) Boomtown Rats
c) The Doors
d) U2

40. What Irish group recorded "Banana Republic" and "I Don't Like Mondays"?
a) The Boomtown Rats
b) Thin Lizzy
c) The Pretenders
d) The Pogues

41.   What contemporary Irish poet said, ''I began as a poet
       when my roots were crossed with my reading. I think of the
       personal and Irish pieties as vowels, and the literary
       awareness nourished on English as consonants''?
       a) John Montague
       b) Thomas Kinsella
       c) Seamus Heaney
       d) Richard Murphy

42.   What Irishwoman wrote *Castle Rackrent* (1800)?
       a) Lady Gregory
       b) Emily Bronte
       c) Maria Edgeworth
       d) Queen Victoria

43.   What Irish poem concerns the dream of a man who finds
       himself in a court ruled by women and enquiring into the
       state of Irishmen?
       a) *The Battle of Aughrim*
       b) *The Vision*
       c) *The Midnight Court*
       d) *The Nightmare*

44.   What famous Irish short story writer was born in Cork in
       1903?
       a) Sherwood Anderson
       b) James Joyce
       c) Mary Lavin
       d) Frank O'Connor

45.   Who wrote the musical score for the film *Mise Éire* and in-
       spired a revival of interest in Irish traditional music?
       a) Shaun Davey
       b) Sean O'Riada
       c) Christy Moore
       d) Donal Lunny

46. What Irish poet is commemorated by an inscribed bench
     on the Grand Canal near Baggott Street, Dublin?
     a) Brendan Behan
     b) Patrick Kavanagh
     c) John Hewitt
     d) Austin Clarke

47. Who wrote *Borstal Boy*, based on his own experience in a
     English borstal, or young man's prison, where he was sent
     for possessing explosives on entry to Liverpool in 1939?
     a) Eamon de Valera
     b) Brendan Behan
     c) Bobby Sands
     d) Sean MacBride

48. What is hurling?
     a) A method of cooking
     b) The traditional custom of throwing fence posts
     c) The most ancient Irish sport
     d) A winter snow sport

49. What is a *sliothar*?
     a) A violent oath
     b) A ball used in hurling
     c) A threat
     d) A weapon

50. What is a *camán*?
     a) A farm-tool
     b) A lullaby
     c) A hurley, or stick used in hurling
     d) A type of poem

51. Since it first formed an Olympic team in 1924, how many
     gold medals has Ireland won?
     a) None

    b) Four
    c) Two
    d) Twenty

52. How many players are on a Gaelic football team?
    a) Four
    b) Fifteen
    c) Twelve
    d) Ten

53. When was the Gaelic Athletic Association founded, its aim being to promote Irish games?
    a) 1916
    b) 1884
    c) 1970
    d) 1914

54. What was the G.A.A. ban?
    a) A ban on its members playing foreign games, rugby or soccer, for example
    b) A ban on refreshments during matches
    c) A ban on Dublin teams
    d) A ban on matches held on Sunday

55. Besides hurling and Gaelic football, what was the third traditional Gaelic sport that the G.A.A. succeeded in promoting?
    a) Camogie
    b) Soccer
    c) Handball
    d) Ice hockey

56. When was the silent movie *How Molly Malone Made Good* made and why was it distinctive?
    a) 1945
    b) 1935
    c) 1925
    d) 1915

57.   Who directed *Ryan's Daughter* (1970)?
      a) Robert Redford
      b) John Ford
      c) David Lean
      d) John Huston

58.   Where in Ireland was *Ryan's Daughter* filmed?
      a) The Donegal coast
      b) Ardmore Film Studios
      c) Dunquin, county Kerry
      d) Dublin City

59.   Who starred as Finian McLonergan in *Finian's Rainbow* (1968)?
      a) Barry Fitzgerald
      b) Fred Astaire
      c) Darby O'Gill
      d) Bing Crosby

60.   Who starred as Finian's daughter?
      a) Grace Kelly
      b) Maureen O'Hara
      c) Meryl Streep
      d) Petula Clark

61.   In what 1959 movie about the early I.R.A. did James Cagney star?
      a) *Cal*
      b) *Shake Hands with the Devil*
      c) *The Last Hurrah*
      d) *Mise Éire*

62.   What novel by Bernard MacLaverty became a movie in 1984?
      a) *The Wild Geese*
      b) *My Oedipus Complex*

c) *The Lamb*
d) *Cal*

63. Who directed *The Quiet Man* (1952)?
a) John Wayne
b) John Ford
c) Dan O'Herlihy
d) George M. Cohan

64. In *The Quiet Man*, who played the part of Sean Thornton, the former boxer?
a) John Wayne
b) Jack Dempsey
c) Gregory Peck
d) Anthony Quinn

65. Who co-starred with Robert Mitchum in *A Terrible Beauty* (1960), set in Northern Ireland during World War II?
a) Tyrone Power
b) Paul Newman
c) Peter O'Toole
d) Richard Harris

66. Who starred as Frank Skeffington, an Irish-American political boss, in *The Last Hurrah* (1958)?
a) Charles Laughton
b) James Michael Curley
c) Spencer Tracey
d) Bob Hoskins

67. Who won an Oscar in 1935 for his direction of *The Informer*?
a) David Lean
b) John Ford
c) George Stevens
d) John O'Hara

68. On whose novel was *The Informer* based?
    a) James Joyce's
    b) Frank O'Connor's
    c) Liam O'Flaherty's
    d) Leon Uris's

69. Who starred as Parnell in the movie of that name in 1937?
    a) John Boycott
    b) Errol Flynn
    c) James Cagney
    d) Clark Gable

70. What famous Irish-American actor starred in the movie version of *The Plough and the Stars* (1936)?
    a) Ronald Reagan
    b) James Cagney
    c) Barry Fitzgerald
    d) Dan O'Herlihy

71. Who played the young priest in *Going My Way* (1940)?
    a) Fred Astaire
    b) William Bendix
    c) Barry Fitzgerald
    d) Bing Crosby

72. In what 1949 movie, starring Bing Crosby and Barry Fitzgerald, did the Blarney Stone disappear?
    a) *The Luck of the Irish*
    b) *Darby O'Gill and the Little People*
    c) *Top o' the Morning*
    d) *Finian's Rainbow*

73. In *The Luck of the Irish* (1947), who was the New York journalist who meets a leprechaun?
    a) Humphrey Bogert
    b) Tyrone Power

c) Clark Gable

d) Spencer Tracey

74.   What 1947 movie, set in Ireland of the 1880s, starred
        Stewart Granger?
        a) *The Molly Maguires*
        b) *Parnell*
        c) *The Tycoon*
        d) *Captain Boycott*

75.   What 1959 Disney movie included an Irish storyteller who
        falls down a well?
        a) *Darby O'Gill and the Little People*
        b) *Finian's Rainbow*
        c) *Ryan's Daughter*
        d) *Going My Way*

Answers

1.   b) "The Dead" by James Joyce

2.   b) G. B. Shaw

3.   d) Lady Gregory, to whom Yeats replied, "Leave it on."

4.   a) *The Playboy of the Western World*, by John Millington Synge

5.   a) Sean O'Casey's *The Plough and the Stars*

6.   d) John McGahern

7.   b) All were victims of the Irish Censorship Board.

8.   a) and c) Flann O'Brien and Myles na gCopaleen were both pseudonyms of the writer Brian O'Nolan.

9.   d) Swift

10.   c) Oliver Goldsmith

11.   b) Juno's lament in *Juno and the Paycock*

12.   c) 1916, around the time of the Easter Rising

13.   c) Beckett

14.   d) Three

15.   George Bernard Shaw, William Butler Yeats, Samuel Beckett

16.   b) Murphy, in the novel of that name

17.   c) Handel's Messiah

18.   b) Adam Hewison

19.   b) Peadar Kearney

20.   d) John McCormack

21.   b) Tommy Makem

22.   b) Traditional Irish dances

23.   a) *Riders to the Sea*

24.   b) 1898

25.   c) and d) in Joyce's *Ulysses*

26.   c) *The Dead* was Huston's last film.

27.   b) Joyce's *Ulysses*

28.   a) Leon Uris

29.   a) Yeats's Easter 1916

30.   d) Yeats

31.   b) ''The top of the morning,'' from the poem ''The Exile's Return'' by John Locke—one of the few recorded expressions of this phrase by an Irish person!

32.   c) Siobhan McKenna

33.   d) The legendary beauty and revolutionary, Maud Gonne

34.   b) The Book of Kells

35.   a) Wilde's

36.   d) *The Cattle Raid of Cooley*—in Irish *Táin Bo Cualnge*

37.   a) From ''In Memory of W. B. Yeats,'' by W. H. Auden

38.   a) A tambourine made of dried sheepskin stretched tightly

39.   a) Thin Lizzy

40.   a) The Boomtown Rats

41.   c) Seamus Heaney

42.   c) Maria Edgeworth

43.   c) *The Midnight Court*, by Brian Merriman

44.　d)　Frank O'Connor, the pseudonym of Michael O'Donovan

45.　b)　Sean O'Riada

46.　b)　Patrick Kavanagh, author of "Lines Written on a Seat on the Grand Canal"

47.　b)　Brendan Behan

48.　c)　Hurling is the most ancient Irish sport.

49.　b)　The ball used in hurling

50.　a)　A hurley, the stick used in hurling

51.　b)　Four: Patrick O'Callaghan (Hammer Throw), 1928 and 1932; Robert Tisdall (400m Hurdles), 1932; and Ron Delaney (1500m), 1956

52.　b)　Fifteen

53.　b)　1884

54.　a)　A ban on the playing of foreign games by its members

55.　c)　Handball

56.　d)　The film, one of the earliest movies with an Irish subject, was made in 1915.

57.　c)　David Lean

58.　c)　Dunquin, county Kerry

59.　b)　Fred Astaire

60.   d) Petula Clark

61.   b) *Shake Hands with the Devil*

62.   d) *Cal*

63.   b) John Ford directed the movie, filmed in Cong, county Mayo.

64.   a) John Wayne

65.   d) Richard Harris

66.   c) Spencer Tracey

67.   b) John Ford

68.   c) Liam O'Flaherty's

69.   d) Clark Gable

70.   c) Barry Fitzgerald

71.   d) Bing Crosby

72.   c) *Top o' the Morning*

73.   b) Tyrone Power

74.   d) Captain Boycott

75.   a) *Darby O'Gill and the Little People*

Dublin

"The town is as full as ever of 'characters,' all created by each other."

Wilfred Sheed

1. Who founded Dublin in 988 A.D.?
     a) The Vikings
     b) The Celts
     c) The Normans
     d) Henry II of England

2. The name Dublin comes from the Irish *Dubh Linn*, which means what?
     a) Dark Rose
     b) City of the Gates
     c) Black Pool
     d) Crossing at the Ford

3. What is the population of Dublin city?
     a) 1,500,000
     b) 915,000
     c) 66,000
     d) 3,000,000

4. Who wrote, "In Dublin you have conviviality, but no friendship. And Dublin will give you loneliness, too—but no solitude"?
    a) Oscar Wilde
    b) G. B. Shaw
    c) James Connolly
    d) Brendan Behan

5. Who said in 1985 that "Dublin used to be one of the prettiest [cities] in Europe and now it's a shambolical mess. . . Not only is the city increasingly brutalized but the people in it have lost their old openness and that is a lot to do with the destruction of the city. Please stop destroying Dublin"?
    a) Charles Haughey
    b) Bono
    c) Garret Fitzgerlad
    d) Bob Geldof

6. Who said of Dublin, "Scribal implements are venerated—there are pen shops in Dublin, as there are stores in New York consecrated to the grand piano"?
    a) Lady Gregory
    b) Hugh Kenner
    c) Henry James
    d) James Joyce

7. Who was the first Catholic Lord Mayor of Dublin?
    a) Charles Stewart Parnell
    b) Jim Larkin
    c) Padraig Pearse
    d) Daniel O'Connell

8. Who founded Trinity College?
    a) Walter Raleigh
    b) Edmund Spenser
    c) William Shakespeare
    d) Queen Elizabeth I

9. Catholic University was founded in 1854 and became University College Dublin in 1882. Who was its first rector after the change?
   a) Cardinal Newman
   b) Oliver Goldsmith
   c) Edmund Burke
   d) G. K. Chesterton

10. Where is the Book of Kells displayed?
   a) The National Museum
   b) The National Gallery
   c) Dublin Castle
   d) Trinity College Library

11. Where is the National Gallery of Ireland located?
   a) Grafton Street
   b) Merrion Square
   c) O'Connell Street
   d) Dawson Street

12. Who bequeathed one third of his estate to the National Gallery, claiming that he received his education there?
   a) W. B. Yeats
   b) James Joyce
   c) George Bernard Shaw
   d) Samuel Beckett

13. What is the name of the home of the National Parliament?
   a) Leinster House
   b) Dublin Castle
   c) Belfield
   d) Mansion House

14. The architect of what American building was strongly influenced by Leinster House?
   a) The White House

b) The Empire State Building
c) Boston State House
d) Treasury Building

15. The main facade of Trinity College faces onto what famous square?
   a) College Green
   b) Stephen's Green
   c) Parnell Square
   d) Merrion Square

16. Dublin's first cinema, the Volta, opened in 1909. Who was its manager?
   a) Lady Gregory
   b) James Joyce
   c) Oscar Wilde
   d) Buck Mulligan

17. What was the home of the English viceroy in Ireland until the establishment of the Free State in 1922?
   a) Christ Church
   b) Dublin Castle
   c) Leinster House
   d) Malahide Castle

18. Who is buried in St. Patrick's Cathedral, where savage indignation can no longer lacerate his heart?
   a) James Joyce
   b) Jonathan Swift
   c) W. B. Yeats
   d) Oscar Wilde

19. Opposite the main facade of Trinity College is the central office of the Bank of Ireland. Built in 1729, it is the former home of what historical institution?
   a) The National Gallery

b) The National Library
c) The Irish Parliament
d) The National Museum

20. Christ Church contains the tomb of what invader of Ireland?
    a) Erik Eriksson
    b) Robert Bruce
    c) Strongbow
    d) Henry II

21. When did brewing of Guinness begin in Dublin?
    a) 1869
    b) 1769
    c) 1969
    d) 1809

22. How many pints of stout does Guinness's fermenting vessel ferment at one brewing?
    a) 1,406,000
    b) 502,000
    c) 2,304,000
    d) 421,000

23. What is the former name of O'Connell Street?
    a) Drogheda Street
    b) Sackville Street
    c) Grafton Street
    d) Duke Street

24. When was Nelson's Pillar in O'Connell Street destroyed by an explosion?
    a) 1966
    b) 1986
    c) 1866
    d) 1916

25. What was the main stronghold of the 1916 Easter Rising?
    a) O'Connell Bridge
    b) Dublin Castle
    c) General Post Office
    d) Leinster House

26. What is the name of the G.A.A. park in Dublin, where the All-Ireland championships are played?
    a) Stephen's Green
    b) Croke Park
    c) Gaelic Stadium
    d) College Green

27. Within the last twenty-five years, Dublin has lost what percentage of its Georgian architecture?
    a) 10 percent
    b) 40 percent
    c) 5 percent
    d) 95 percent

28. What theater was established by Hilton Edwards and Michael MacLiammoir in 1929?
    a) The Peacock
    b) The Abbey
    c) The Gaiety
    d) The Gate

29. In what Dublin church can you shake hands with a dead crusader?
    a) Christ Church
    b) St. Michan's Church
    c) St. Patrick's Cathedral
    d) The Pro-Cathedral

30. When is the Dublin Horse Show held?
    a) July

   b) December
   c) August
   d) March

31.   When is the Dublin Theatre Festival?
      a) October
      b) March
      c) June
      d) May

32.   Of what event in Dublin's history was it said, ''It is the first
      time it has happened since Moscow, the first time that a
      capital has been burnt since then''?
      a) The Irish Civil War
      b) The accidental bombing during World War II
      c) The 1916 Rising
      d) The last Viking raid

33.   Where does the famous literary debate in the Scylla and
      Charybdis chapter of *Ulysses* take place?
      a) The National Library
      b) Trinity College
      c) The National Gallery
      d) University College Dublin

34.   What pub, still located on Duke Street, does Leopold Bloom
      visit in *Ulysses*?
      a) The Brazen Head
      b) The Bailey
      c) Davy Byrne's
      d) McDaid's

35.   When is Bloomsday?
      a) June 14
      b) June 4
      c) June 16
      d) July 16

36.   Where is Joyce's Tower, now the James Joyce Museum,
       located?
          a) Sandymount
          b) Grafton Street
          c) Sandycove
          d) Rathmines

37.   On what day did James Joyce first meet Nora Barnacle?
          a) June 16, 1910
          b) June 16, 1905
          c) June 16, 1904
          d) June 16, 1914

38.   The door of Bloom's home, 7 Eccles Street, is today in what
       Dublin haunt?
          a) Trinity College
          b) The National Library
          c) The Bailey Pub
          d) The G.P.O.

39.   What Irish writer was born on Dorset Street, Dublin, in
       1889?
          a) James Joyce
          b) Sean O'Casey
          c) Samuel Beckett
          d) Flann O'Brien

40.   The author of *Dracula* was born in 1847 in Marino, Dublin.
       Who was he?
          a) Bram Stoker
          b) Percy Shelley
          c) William Frankenstein
          d) Fritz Lang

41.   For what newspaper did Myles na gCopaleen write regular articles?
     a) The *Irish Independent*
     b) The *Irish Times*
     c) The *London Times*
     c) The *Irish Press*

42.   What Dublin-based record label is sponsored by the rock group U2?
     a) Mother Records
     b) A & M
     c) Claddagh Records
     d) Tower Records

Answers

1.   a) The Vikings

2.   c) Black Pool

3.   b) 915,000

4.   d) Brendan Behan

5.   d) Bob Geldof

6.   b) Hugh Kenner

7.   d) Daniel O'Connell, the nineteenth-century politician and champion of Catholic Emancipation

8.   d) Queen Elizabeth founded Trinity College in 1592.

9.   a) Cardinal Newman

10.   d) Trinity College Library

11.   b) Merrion Square

12.   c) G. B. Shaw

13.   a) Leinster House

14.   a) The White House

15.   a) College Green

16.   b) James Joyce

17.   b) Dublin Castle

18.   b) Jonathan Swift, dean of St. Patrick's from 1713 to 1745

19.   c) Ireland's only parliament under British Rule, 1782 to 1800, was located here.

20.   c) Strongbow, the leader of the Norman invasion in the 1170s

21.   b) 1769

22.   c) 2,304,000 pints

23.   a) Drogheda Street and b) Sackville Street

24.   a) 1966

25.   c) The G.P.O. on O'Connell Street

26.   b) Croke Park

27. b) 40 percent

28. d) The Gate

29. b) St. Michan's

30. c) August

31. a) October

32. c) The 1916 Rising

33. a) The National Library

34. c) Davy Byrne's

35. c) June 16

36. c) Sandycove

37. c) June 16, 1904, later commemorated by Joyce as the day on which *Ulysses* takes place

38. c) The Bailey

39. b) Sean O'Casey

40. a) Bram Stoker

41. b) The *Irish Times*

42. a) Mother Records

Ireland Today

"Irishness is not primarily a question of birth or blood or language; it is the condition of being involved in the Irish situation, and usually of being mauled by it."

Conor Cruise O'Brien

1.　　In the 1981 census, what was the population of the Republic of Ireland?
    a) 3.5 million
    b) 1 million
    c) 10 million
    d) 6.5 million

2.　　Approximately what percentage of Ireland's population is under twenty-five?
    a) 10 percent
    b) 20 percent
    c) 50 percent
    d) 75 percent

3.　　In the 1981 census, what percentage of the population of the Irish Republic was Roman Catholic?
    a) 93 percent
    b) 80 percent

c) 50 percent
d) 75 percent

4. What percentage of the Republic's population is Jewish?
    a) 5 percent
    b) 6 percent
    c) 2 percent
    d) .06 percent

5. In Northern Ireland, what percentage of the population is Roman Catholic by birth?
    a) 30 percent
    b) 20 percent
    c) 50 percent
    d) 80 percent

6. What is Ireland's official color?
    a) Blue
    b) Orange
    c) White
    d) Green

7. What is the oldest official symbol of Ireland?
    a) The Shamrock
    b) The Harp
    c) The Celtic Cross
    d) The Wolfhound

8. What quasinational institution adopted the harp as its symbol in 1862?
    a) Aer Lingus
    b) Guinness
    c) The weaving industry
    d) Waterford Glass

9.   Who introduced the tricolor into Ireland?
      a) Eamon de Valera
      b) Wolfe Tone
      c) Thomas F. Meagher
      d) Robert Emmet

10.   When was the tricolor recognized as the official flag of the
      Republic?
      a) 1949
      b) 1937
      c) 1916
      d) 1922

11.   Adopted as the National Anthem in 1926, "The Soldier's
      Song" displaced what earlier Fenian anthem?
      a) "The Wearing of the Green"
      b) "The Dear Little Shamrock"
      c) "God Save Ireland"
      d) "O Danny Boy"

12.   When did Ireland become a member of the European
      Economic Community (E.E.C.)?
      a) 1910
      b) 1973
      c) Never
      d) 1953

13.   When was Ireland admitted to the United Nations?
      a) 1965
      b) 1985
      c) 1955
      d) 1922

14.   What is the total area of Ireland (including Northern
      Ireland)?
      a) 32,595 square miles

b) 140,621 square miles
c) 62,941 square miles
d) 17,369 square miles

15. To which of the following states is Ireland nearest in size?
    a) Oklahoma
    b) Ohio
    c) Maine
    d) Rhode Island

16. What fraction of Ireland's total land area is the political entity Northern Ireland?
    a) One tenth
    b) One sixth
    c) One third
    d) Half

17. What is the greatest length of the island of Ireland, from north to south?
    a) 33 miles
    b) 302 miles
    c) 79 miles
    d) 522 miles

18. How many houses does the national parliament (*Oireachtas*) contain?
    a) One
    b) Four
    c) Ten
    d) Two

19. Name them.

20. Who is the *Taoiseach*?
    a) The President
    b) The Prime Minister

c) The Official Government Entertainer
d) The Minister for Foreign Affairs

21. What are the most and second most common surnames in
     Ireland?
     a) Kelly, O'Connor
     b) O'Sullivan, O'Connell
     c) McCarthy, Byrne
     d) Murphy, Kelly

22. What does the prefix "Mac" literally mean?
     a) From
     b) Son of
     c) Wife of
     d) Belonging to

23. Which of the following is not an Irish political party?
     a) Fianna Fail
     b) Fine Gael
     c) Liberal
     d) Labour

24. What, under the Irish Constitution, is Ireland's first official
     language?
     a) Irish
     b) Gaelic
     c) English
     d) Irish bull

25. Whose picture is featured on the Irish ten-pound banknote?
     a) W. B. Yeats
     b) Eamon de Valera
     c) Jonathan Swift
     d) George Washington

26. Who was the only person ever to win both the Nobel Peace Prize and the Lenin Peace Prize?
    a) Mairead Corrigan
    b) Sean MacBride
    c) Conor Cruise O'Brien
    d) Lech Walesa

27. When was divorce made legal in Ireland?
    a) 1922
    b) 1985
    c) Never
    d) 1963

28. In 1987 unemployment in the Republic of Ireland passed what figure for the first time?
    a) 100,000
    b) 250,000
    c) 10,000
    d) 5,000

29. What sea is officially the most radioactive in the world due to the discharge from Sellafield (Windscale) nuclear plant?
    a) The North Sea
    b) Atlantic Ocean
    c) The Black Sea
    d) The Irish Sea

30. On what days are Irish pubs closed?
    a) Never
    b) Every Sunday
    c) Good Friday and Christmas Day
    d) Ash Wednesday and Good Friday

31. When was Aer Lingus, Ireland's national airline, established?
    a) 1986

b) 1936
c) 1916
d) 1926

32. How many pubs are in the Republic of Ireland?
    a) 1,463
    b) 3,596
    c) 9,939
    d) 192

33. How many international airports does Ireland have?
    a) Five
    b) None
    c) One
    d) Two

34. With Ireland's population at 3.5 million, what is the approx-
     imate ratio of pubs to people?
    a) 1 to 2,000 people
    b) 1 to 150 people
    c) 1 to 1,000 people
    d) 1 to 350 people

35. How old is Ireland's ban on divorce?
    a) 1,000 years
    b) 200 years
    c) 50 years
    d) 500 years

36. When did the first package tour from the United States ar-
     rive in Ireland?
    a) 1925
    b) 1935
    c) 1895
    d) 1945

37.   What is Ireland's biggest edible export?
       a) Milk
       b) Beef
       c) Butter
       d) Guinness

38.   What Irish city is famous for its crystal?
       a) Waterford
       b) Cavan
       c) Galway
       d) All of the above

39.   How many Irish-born people live in Britain?
       a) 100,000
       b) 850,000
       c) 50,000
       d) 200,000

40.   What is the conservative government estimate of emigra-
       tion in 1985–1986?
       a) 10,000
       b) 31,000
       c) 5,000
       d) 20,000

41.   What has been Ireland's greatest period of emigration in
       the twentieth century?
       a) The 1980s
       b) The 1950s
       c) The 1930s
       d) The 1910s

42.   How many morning daily newspapers are published in the
       Irish Republic?
       a) Three
       b) Four

    c) Two
    d) Six

43.   How many counties are in the Republic of Ireland?
    a) 26
    b) 32
    c) 25
    d) 10

44.   Of how many counties does Northern Ireland consist?
    a) Two
    b) Ten
    c) Six
    d) Nine

45.   What county is known as the Rebel County?
    a) Cork
    b) Waterford
    c) Antrim
    d) Derry

46.   What county is known as The Kingdom?
    a) Armagh
    b) Dublin
    c) Meath
    d) Kerry

47.   What county is known as the Banner County?
    a) Galway
    b) Clare
    c) Mayo
    d) Tyrone

48.   What is the largest Irish county?
    a) Dublin
    b) Cork

c) Galway
d) Meath

49.   Where does Ireland rank among other nations in area?
        a) 110th
        b) 20th
        c) 1,000th
        d) 500th

50.   What percentage of voters voted no to divorce in the 1986 referendum?
        a) 63 percent
        b) 52 percent
        c) 99 percent
        d) 28 percent

51.   Whose picture appears on the Irish twenty-pound banknote?
        a) W. B. Yeats
        b) Oscar Wilde
        c) John F. Kennedy
        d) Maud Gonne

Answers

1. a) 3.5 million

2. c) 50 percent

3. a) 93 percent

4. d) .06 percent

5. a) 30 percent

6. a) Blue, the color of the field in Ireland's coat of arms

7. b) The traditional Celtic harp

8. b) Guinness

9. c) Meagher, in 1848

10.   b) 1937

11.   c) "God Save Ireland"

12.   b) 1973

13.   c) 1955

14.   a) 32,595 square miles

15.   c) The area of Maine is 33,215 square miles.

16.   b) One sixth, or 5,459 square miles

17.   b) 302 miles

18.   d) Two

19.   The House of Representatives or *Dáil* and the Senate or *Seanad*

20.   b) The prime minister, who is the leader of the majority political party

21.   d) Murphy and Kelly

22.   b) Son of

23.   c) Liberal

24.   a) Irish—English is Ireland's second official language while Gaelic, as a term for the Irish language, is not used within Ireland.

25.   c) Jonathan Swift

26.   b) Sean MacBride, who won the Nobel Prize in 1974 and the Lenin Prize in 1977

27.   c) Divorce is not permitted under Irish law.

28.   b) 250,000 out of a population of 3.5 million

29.   d) The Irish Sea

30.   c) Good Friday and Christmas Day

31.   b) 1936

32.   c) 9,939

33.   a) Five: Shannon, Cork, Knock, Dublin and Belfast

34.   d) 1 to 350 people

35.   c) The ban was first imposed in the 1937 constitution.

36.   c) 1895

37.   b) Beef currently constitutes 25 percent of Ireland's total food exports.

38.   d) All three cities

39.   b) 850,000, of whom 650,000 were born in the Republic

40.   b) 31,000

41.   b) The 1950s, but the figures for the 1980s continue to rise.

42.   b) Four: the *Irish Independent*, the *Irish Press*, the *Irish Times* and the *Cork Examiner*

Ireland Today—Answers

43. a) 26

44. c) Six: Antrim, Armagh, Derry, Down, Fermanagh and Tyrone

45. a) Cork

46. d) Kerry

47. b) Clare

48. b) Cork

49. a) 110th, between Sierra Leone and Sri Lanka

50. a) 63 percent

51. a) W. B. Yeats

Words

"English is a world language and we are lucky to have it, particularly as we have embroidered it with the tweedy fol-de-lols and porter stains which are unmistakeably Irish and proud of it."

Myles na gCopaleen

The Irish Contribution to English

1. What word derives from the name of an English landlord in Ireland in the 1870s who received hostile treatment from his tenants?
    a) Ostracize
    b) Ignore
    c) Boycott
    d) Coventry

2. What word, describing the Irish way of speaking, entered the English language directly from the Irish word for shoe?
    a) Gaelic
    b) Blarney
    c) Blather
    d) Brogue

3. What word meaning "plentiful" derives from the Irish words for enough?

   a) Loads
   b) Galore
   c) Ample
   d) Bountiful

4. This word, derived from the Irish word for crying, describes the Irish tradition of funeral laments. What is it?
   a) Kerning
   b) Keening
   c) Blathering
   d) Waking

5. What beverage, traditionally associated with Ireland, means, in its Irish form, ''water of life''?
   a) Tea
   b) Whiskey
   c) Porter
   d) Poteen

6. What word for a decrepit dwelling is said to derive from the Irish words for old house?
   a) Shack
   b) Cabin
   c) Hut
   d) Shanty

7. What town in county Dublin gave its name to the description of a brawl?
   a) Brouhaha
   b) Ballyhooly
   c) Donnybrook
   d) Toodoo

8. What Irish surname became the term for a type of execution?
   a) Burke

b) Boycott

c) Lynch

d) Guillotine

9. This name, describing the supporters of an English political party, derives from the Irish word for pursue.
   a) Liberal
   b) Tory
   c) Whig
   d) Orangemen

10. The word "hooligan" derives from the name of what famous Irish family in London in the 1890s?
    a) The Hoopers
    b) The Houlihans
    c) The Horgans
    d) The McCarthys

11. The word for an area where turf can be cut derives from the Irish word for soft. What is it?
    a) Peat
    b) Marsh
    c) Bog
    d) Swamp

12. What word derives from the ancient name for a Celtic poet?
    a) Songster
    b) Laureate
    c) Bard
    d) Blatherer

13. What word meaning small fragments is a direct transliteration of the equivalent Irish word?
    a) Sherds
    b) Smithereens
    c) Flotsam
    d) Bits

14. ''Tory'' was first used in the late seventeeth century to describe the Irish supporters of whom?
    a) Oliver Cromwell
    b) Bonnie Price Charles
    c) King James II
    d) William of Orange

15. *Fáinne* (fawn-yuh), the Irish word that gave us "phoney," describes what piece of jewelry (reputedly because Irish emigrants to New York sold brass pieces, claiming them to be gold)?
    a) A ring
    b) A bracelet
    c) A locket
    d) A watch

16. What word comes from the name of the woods in county Wicklow from which oak clubs were believed to come?
    a) Louisville Slugger
    b) Hurley
    c) Shillelagh
    d) Thumper

17. The Irish word *seamrog* was adopted into English in the sixteenth century as what?
    a) Sham
    b) Rogue
    c) Phoney conman
    d) Shamrock

18. What is the name of the early Irish runic alphabet?
    a) Ogham
    b) Uncial
    c) Gaelic
    d) Roman

19. What word meaning "smooth talk" is also the name of a castle in Cork?
    a) Blarney
    b) Blather
    c) Killarney
    d) Plawmaws

20. What word meaning "noisy preliminary publicity" is said to derive from the name of an Irish village?
    a) Blarney
    b) Fuss
    c) Donnybrook
    d) Ballyhoo

21. Where is this exceptionally talkative village located?
    a) County Dublin
    b) County Kerry
    c) County Cork
    d) County Antrim

22. What word meaning "confused din" or "disturbance" may derive from the Irish war cry *abú*?
    a) Ablutions
    b) Ballyhoo
    c) Hubbub
    d) Rhubarb

23. This word meaning "noise" or "to bewilder with noise" derives from the Irish word for deaf. What is it?
    a) Din
    b) Bother
    c) Blather
    d) Addle

24. What Irish word translates as woman of the fairies?
    a) Brighid

b) Nun

c) Banshee

d) Pooka

25. What word originally meant a laborer, but now is used to describe a mean fellow or rascal?

    a) *Amadán*

    b) Paddy

    c) Spalpeen

    d) Eejit

26. What Irish word for an illicit beverage means literally "small pot"?

    a) Boreen

    b) Poteen

    c) Liquor

    d) Nixer

27. If someone is described as "maggalore" then the person is what?

    a) Witty

    b) Drunk

    c) Talkative

    d) Ill

28. What is a shebeen?

    a) A pig's foot, cooked in brine

    b) An Irish diva

    c) The wife of an extraterrestrial being

    d) An illegal public house

29. What, in Irish history, is a kern?

    a) A light-armed Irish foot-soldier

    b) A house of ill repute

    c) A printing term

    d) A barrel of grain that, during the Famine, was withheld by British authorities

30.   What Irish word was adopted by nineteenth century ar-
        chaeologists to describe Bronze or Iron Age lake dwellings?
        a) *Curragh*
        b) *Cavin*
        c) *Loughus*
        d) *Crannog*

31.   In the phrase "gift of the gab," what does gab literally mean?
        a) Gaelic
        b) Money
        c) Language
        d) Mouth

A Smattering of Gaelic

32.   If you were in an Irish pub with someone who was described
        as *flathúil* (fla-*hool*), how would your glass be?
        a) Empty
        b) Overflowing
        c) Half-full
        d) Gone

33.   If money in Ireland is described as *flúirseach* (flew-shirk),
        it means it is what?
        a) Getting low
        b) Barely remembered
        c) Due to arrive any day
        d) Plentiful

34.   If someone's words are *plamás* (pluh-*moss*), then they are
        what?
        a) To be fully believed
        b) To be censored
        c) To be treated with scepticism but enjoyed
        d) To be translated

35.   If your lecture is said to be *ráiméis* (raw-maish), what does that mean?
        a) You won over your audience.
        b) It has been dismissed as nonsense.
        c) No one understood you.
        d) You should avoid thrown objects.

36.   To have a lot of *meas* (mass) in someone is to what?
        a) Have invested money in his company
        b) Have a lot of respect for that person
        c) Have shared a religious affiliation
        d) Be closely related

37.   If you are described as having *mí-adh* (mee-aw) what does that mean?
        a) You should immediately buy a lottery ticket.
        b) You should visit a doctor.
        c) You should avoid all risks.
        d) You are well respected.

38.   What is a *currach*?
        a) A small boat made of waterproof material
        b) A piece of clothing
        c) A derogatory term
        d) An Irish house

39.   The *íochtar* (eek-tur) of an Irish family is what?
        a) The eldest child
        b) The youngest child
        c) The wealthiest American relative
        d) The guardian

40.   Which of the following is not a term of endearment?
        a) "Ashtore"
        b) "Macchree"
        c) "Avourneen"
        d) "Whisht"

41. In Ireland a "boreen" is what?
    a) A boring person
    b) A drill
    c) A narrow laneway
    d) A long tunic

42. In Ireland, a *ciotog* (kit-*ogue*) is what?
    a) A bird
    b) A plant
    c) A left-handed person
    d) A type of church

43. The phrase *Erin go bragh* literally means what?
    a) Ireland free
    b) Ireland forever
    c) Ireland's mine
    d) Ireland itself

44. The phrase *céad míle fáilte* (kaid-meela-fallta) literally means what?
    a) A hundred thousand welcomes
    b) Good to see you
    c) You have permission to come in
    d) Three thousand miles away

45. To describe someone's *blas* is to refer to one's what?
    a) Accent in speaking the Irish language
    b) Ancestry
    c) Income
    d) Sense of dress

46. If you are told that you have won the lottery, "mor-yah," what does that mean?
    a) You should celebrate.
    b) You shouldn't believe the news.
    c) You will have to share it.
    d) You will pay most in tax.

47. On an Irish farm you may hear a call to hens that sounds like "chook, chook." What is being said?
   a) Beware, a visitor
   b) Come here, come here
   c) Time for food
   d) You stupid bird

Some Slang

48. What is the significance of the following extract from Arthur Young's *A Tour in Ireland* (1780)? "The paddies were swimming their horses in the sea to cure the mange, or keep them in health."
   a) The first recorded reference to mange
   b) A comparison to Chinese custom
   c) The first recorded use of "paddy" to describe an Irish person
   d) A traditional superstition

49. What are "quare stuff" and "a drop of the crathure"?
   a) Irish racehorses
   b) Slang names for whiskey or poteen
   c) Names of famous Irish pubs
   d) Slang names for tea and coffee

50. If you are described in Ireland as being "great crack," that means you are what?
   a) Off the wall
   b) Great fun
   c) A laugh a minute
   d) A scream
   e) All of the above

51. From what Irish name does the term "paddy" derive?
   a) Patrick
   b) Padraig

c) Michael

d) Sean

52. In Victorian England the term "paddy" also meant what?
   a) A violent temper tantrum
   b) A Welsh person
   c) A Chinese person
   d) An easy victory

53. In English slang what is a "boglander" or a "bog-trotter"?
   a) A laborer
   b) A cutter of peat moss
   c) An Irishman
   d) A Scottish person

54. Who described the term Irishman as a "pejorative singular"?
   a) Jonathan Swift
   b) Conor Cruise O'Brien
   c) Edward Heath
   d) Flann O'Brien

55. The description of Ireland as "England's umbrella" refers to what?
   a) The political tension
   b) Its frequent rain
   c) Ireland's former colonial status
   d) Its relative size

56. In English slang, "To have an Irishman's dinner" means what?
   a) To eat too much
   b) To be forced to go without an expected meal
   c) To have breakfast
   d) To dine out

57. ''To go to an Irish wedding'' is also an English expression for what?
    a) Emptying a cesspool
    b) An ancient Irish custom
    c) An annual obligation
    d) Receiving a black eye

58. What is an ''Irish welcome''?
    a) Not being welcome
    b) A standing invitation with no restrictions
    c) Tea and scones
    d) A tourist ploy

59. What is ''Irish beauty''?
    a) Two black eyes
    b) Outstanding good looks
    c) A famous Irish racehorse
    d) An Irish ballad

60. What is an ''Irish bull''?
    a) A Holstein
    b) An ancient Irish epic
    c) A statement, the second part of which annuls the first
    d) Blarney

61. What are Munster plums?
    a) Apples
    b) Cabbages
    c) Plums grown in Cork
    d) Potatoes

62. ''Begob,'' ''begorra'' and ''bejabers'' are all what?
    a) Irish characters in plays
    b) Authentic Irish exclamations
    c) Exclamations originating in stage Irish characterisations
    d) Irish euphemisms

Answers

The Irish Contribution to English

1. c) The landlord's name was Captain Boycott.

2. d) The Irish word for shoe is *bróg*.

3. b) Galore, from the Irish *go leor*, adapted in the seventeenth century

4. b) Keening, from the Irish word *caoineadh* (*queen*-uh)

5. b) Whiskey, from the Irish *uisce beatha* (*ish*-kuh *ba*-ha)

6. d) Shanty, from Irish *sean tigh* (shan tig)

7. c) Donnybrook

8.   c) Lynch. Reputedly, this term goes back several centuries to a Lord Mayor of Galway named Lynch, who hanged his own son.

9.   b) Tory, from the Irish *tóraidhe* (tory)

10.   b) The Houlihans

11.   c) Bog

12.   c) Bard

13.   b) Smithereens, in Irish *smithiríní*

14.   c) King James II

15.   a) A ring. Reputedly, Irish immigrants in New York sold brass rings, claiming they were gold.

16.   c) Shillelagh

17.   d) Shamrock

18.   a) Ogham

19.   a) Blarney

20.   d) Ballyhoo, from the village Ballyhooly

21.   c) County Cork

22.   c) Hubbub

23.   b) Bother, from the Irish word *bodhar* (bow-er)

24.   c) Banshee, *bean sídhe* (ban-shee) in Irish

25.   c) Spalpeen, from Irish *spailpín* (spal-peen)

26.   b) Poteen—*pot* and the diminutive *-ín* or een (puh-*cheen*)

27.   b) Drunk, from *maith go leor* meaning "well on" or "good enough"

28.   d) An illegal public house

29.   a) A light-armed Irish foot-soldier

30.   d) *Crannog* (cran-*ogue*)

31.   d) "Gab" or "gob" is Irish slang for mouth.

A Smattering of Gaelic

32.   b) The Irish word *flathúil* literally means "chieftainlike," and came to mean generous or liberal.

33.   d) *Flúirseach* literally means plentiful.

34.   c) *Plamás* means flattery.

35.   b) *Ráiméis* literally means nonsensical talk.

36.   b) *Meas* is the Irish word for respect.

37.   c) *Mí-adh* means bad luck or jinx.

38.   a) A small boat made of waterproof material

39.   b) *Íochtar* literally means lower part or bottom.

40.   d) "Whisht" literally means "be quiet."

41.   c) The Irish word for road is *bóthar.*

42.   c) A left-handed person

43.   b) Ireland forever

44.   a) A hundred thousand welcomes

45.   a) Accent

46.   b) "Mor-yah" comes from *mar sheadh* meaning "as it were," and implies pretense or falsity.

47.   b) "Come here, come here," from *tioc*, the Irish verb "to come"

Some Slang

48.   c) The first recorded use of "paddy"

49.   b) Slang for whiskey or poteen

50.   e) All of the above; the Irish word *craic* literally means fun.

51.   a) and b) Padraig is the Irish form of Patrick.

52.   a) A violent tantrum

53.   c) An Irishman

54.   b) Conor Cruise O'Brien

55.   b) Its frequent rain

56.   b) To be forced to go without an expected meal

57.   a) and d) Emptying a cesspool and receiving a black eye

58.   b) A standing invitation with no restrictions

59.   a) Two black eyes

60.   c) A statement like the following: "I was surprised to learn that Bill Quinn was married in America. I always thought he was dead before he went over there."

61.   d) Potatoes

62.   c) and d)

Food

When food is scarce
And your larder's bare
And no rashers grease your pan
When hunger grows
As your meals grow rare,
A pint of plain is your only man.

Flann O'Brien

1. What is colcannon?
   a) A large cake, traditionally eaten at Christmas
   b) A traditional dish made with seaweed
   c) A type of ammunition
   d) A traditional dish made of potatoes, cabbage, milk and butter

2. When is colcannon traditionally eaten?
   a) Every day
   b) Any day
   c) Halloween
   d) Christmas Day

3. According to the song, what famous Dublin food did Molly Malone sell as she wheeled her wheelbarrow through streets broad and narrow?
   a) Corned beef and cabbage
   b) Oysters

133

c) Cockles and mussels
d) Conkers and mussels

4. What are cockles?
   a) A root vegetable
   b) A type of Dublin potato
   c) A shellfish
   d) Souvenirs

5. When should nettles be picked?
   a) Never
   b) May
   c) December 25
   d) In darkness

6. What are Smiling Murphies?
   a) Pints of stout, brewed in Cork
   b) Creamed potatoes
   c) Pancakes
   d) Potatoes that are floury when boiled

7. What Irish fish is named in Irish legend as the fish of knowledge or *bradán feasa*?
   a) The mackerel
   b) The whale
   c) The salmon
   d) The cod

8. Who, according to Irish legend, is said to have gained the wisdom of the ages when he touched this roasting fish and licked his thumb?
   a) Cuchulainn
   b) The leader of the Spanish Armada
   c) Eamon de Valera
   d) Fionn Mac Cumhail (Finn MacCool)

9.   What city is famous for its oysters and oyster festival?
        a) Galway
        b) Ballyporeen
        c) Kilkenny
        d) Baile na Gall

10.   What is considered to be Ireland's most popular traditional
      dish?
        a) Guinness
        b) Curried chips
        c) Tripe
        d) Boiled bacon and cabbage

11.   What is a true Dubliner's Saturday supper?
        a) Lobster
        b) Potatoes
        c) Coddle
        d) Fish and chips

12.   What are crubeens (*crúibíns*)?
        a) Pigs' feet
        b) Baked beans
        c) Bread puddings
        d) Illegal pubs

13.   These are the ingredients for what traditional dish?
            2 lbs. lean mutton pieces
            1 lb. onions, sliced
            2 lbs. potatoes, peeled and sliced
            1 tablespoon parsley, chopped
            Salt and pepper
            Pinch of thyme
            2½ cups of stock
        a) Chili
        b) Steak and kidney pie
        c) Irish Stew
        d) Boxty

14.　Which of the following is incorrect in making Irish Stew?
　　　a) Too much liquid
　　　b) Adding carrots
　　　c) Cooking at too high a temperature
　　　d) Adding pearl barley

15.　Who said, "There is in every cook's opinion/No savoury dish without an onion/But lest your kissing should be spoiled/The onion must be thoroughly boiled"?
　　　a) Jonathan Swift
　　　b) Julia Child
　　　c) Elizabeth I
　　　d) Padraig Pearse

16.　What Irish beverage is traditionally added to a beef stew?
　　　a) Bailey's
　　　b) Coffee
　　　c) Whiskey
　　　d) Porter

17.　Which meat is traditionally eaten on St. Stephen's Day?
　　　a) Spiced Beef
　　　b) Boiled bacon
　　　c) Left-over turkey
　　　d) Goose

18.　What is boxty?
　　　a) The day after Christmas
　　　b) An Easter cake
　　　c) A traditional dish made with raisins
　　　d) A traditional dish made with potatoes

19.　What is tripe?
　　　a) A nonsensical menu
　　　b) Leftovers
　　　c) Pigs' feet
　　　d) The lining of a sheep's or cow's stomach

20.   With what Irish city is tripe traditionally associated?
       a) Cork
       b) Dingle
       c) Galway
       d) Dublin

21.   In the fourth chapter of Joyce's *Ulysses*, what breakfast food
       does Leopold Bloom prepare for himself?
       a) Pancakes
       b) Kidneys
       c) Porridge
       d) Potatoes

22.   In Ireland, tea is the name for what?
       a) A hot beverage
       b) An evening meal, usually of light fare
       c) A piece of golf equipment
       d) Hot weather

23.   For what high tea dish are the following ingredients used?
           ½ lb. flour
           ½ teaspoon salt
           ½ teaspoon bicarbonate of soda
           2 eggs, well beaten
           1½ cups buttermilk or fresh milk

       a) Buttermilk pancakes
       b) An Irish fry
       c) Potato cakes
       d) Jam scones

24.   When are pancakes traditionally eaten?
       a) Shrove Tuesday, the day before Lent begins
       b) Good Friday
       c) Every Sunday
       d) Never

25. For what famous Irish food are the following ingredients used?

> 8 oz. white flour
> 8 oz. wholemeal flour
> 1 teaspoon baking soda
> 3 teaspoons baking powder
> 2 teaspoons salt
> 1 beaten egg
> 2½ cups of sour milk
> Beaten egg or milk (to glaze)

   a) Muffins
   b) Bagels
   c) Brown soda bread
   d) Gingerbread

26. These are the directions for what Irish beverage?

> Warm a stemmed whiskey glass. Put into it sugar to taste. Add strong, very hot coffee, to within 1½ inches of the top, and stir well. (Place a teaspoon in the glass before adding the coffee to avoid cracking.) Add whiskey to fill up to ½ inch below the top. Hold a teaspoon with its curved side up, across the glass and pour one teaspoon of lightly whipped cream over it. Do not stir, but drink at once. (And start again!)

   a) Guinness
   b) Irish Mist
   c) Irish coffee
   d) Hot Bailey's

27. What is the greatest error in making an Irish coffee?
   a) Not warming the glass
   b) Forgetting the whiskey
   c) Stirring the final product
   d) Too much sugar

28. What is drisheen?
    a) A meat fat
    b) A pudding made with sheep's blood
    c) Bacon
    d) Mashed potato

29. With what area is drisheen traditionally associated?
    a) Cork
    b) Northern Ireland
    c) Rural areas
    d) Wet areas

30. What is a traditional Irish cure for colds, influenza and cold days?
    a) Ice-cubes
    b) Punch
    c) Sleep
    d) Guinness

31.   Did you treat your Mary-Ann
        To dulse and yellow man
        At the old Lammas Fair at Ballycastle-oh?

    What is "yellow man"?

    a) Traditional Irish toffee
    b) Cotton candy
    c) A drink made with whiskey
    d) Fried bananas

32. What is dulse?
    a) A place in Ireland
    b) Edible seaweed
    c) Tripe
    d) A hot drink

33. What cake is associated with Halloween?

a) Christmas cake
b) Barm brack
c) Soda bread
d) Cheesecake

34.   What tea-time dish is traditionally served with jam?
a) Sausages
b) Drisheen
c) Dried toast
d) Scones

35.   Who is reputed to have brought garlic and onions to Ireland?
a) The Vikings
b) American tourists
c) The Spanish
d) The Italians

36.   What is the basic ingredient for what Jonathan Swift called "a most delicious, nourishing and wholesome food, whether stewed, roasted, baked, or boiled, and I make no doubt that it will be equally served in a fricassee, or a ragout?"
a) A young healthy Irish child
b) A goose
c) Garlic
d) Onions

37.   Who is reputed to have brought the potato to Ireland?
a) Sir Walter Raleigh
b) St. Patrick
c) The Vikings
d) The Normans

38.   Dublin Bay prawns are really what?
a) Prawns
b) A type of Norway lobster

c) Vegetables

d) Galway Bay prawns

39.   What is the traditional Christmas dinner bird in Ireland?
       a) Ptarmigan
       b) Pheasant
       c) Goose
       d) Turkey

40.   What is traditionally eaten with Christmas pudding?
       a) Gravy
       b) Egg custard
       c) Salt
       d) Brandy butter

Answers

1.   d) Irish *cal ceann fhionn*, literally "white-haired cabbage"

Did you ever eat Colcannon
When 'twas made from thickened cream,
And the kale and praties blended
Like the picture in a dream?
Did you ever take a forkful
And dip it in the lake
Of the clover-flavoured butter
That your mother used to make?

Colcannon
Peel and boil four lbs. of potatoes. Drain, mash until smooth. Add six chopped scallions to 10 oz. of milk and bring to boil. Add to potatoes and beat well until fluffy. Beat in one lb. cooked curly kale or savoy cabbage (finely chopped) and one oz. butter. Reheat if necessary. Serve with butter.

2.   c) Halloween

3.   c) Cockles and mussels

Cream of Mussel Soup

2 cups mussels (washed thoroughly)
1 quart cold water
2 oz. butter
1 oz. flour
1 cup cream
Salt and pepper

Heat mussels in a dry frying pan until the shells open. Shell and beard mussels. In a saucepan melt butter, add flour and fry for 1–2 minutes. Remove from heat and stir in water, plus any liquid from frying pan. Add salt and pepper, bring to the boil, cover and simmer for ten minutes. Remove from heat. Stir in mussels and cream. Serve immediately.

4.   c) A shellfish

5.   b) According to a traditional receipe for blood purification, three meals of nettles should be eaten in May, a tradition that originates from the shortage of greens in May.

Nettle Soup

2½ cups nettle tops (washed a number of times)
1 oz. butter
1 oz. oatmeal
2½ cups water, stock or milk
Salt and pepper to taste

Chop nettles finely. Melt butter, sprinkle in oatmeal and fry until golden brown. Stir in water, stock or milk. Bring to the boil, stirring continously. Add nettles, salt and pepper. Bring to the boil. Lower heat and simmer for thirty to forty-five minutes.

6.   d) The potato has various nicknames, including spud, pratie and Murphy.

7.   c) The salmon

8.   d) Fionn. Leader of the Fianna—legendary Irish warriors.

9.   a) Galway

10.   d) Boiled bacon and cabbage

11.   c) Coddle

Coddle

¼ lb. streaky bacon (chopped)
¼ lb. pork sausages (whole)
¾ lb. onions (coarsely chopped)
2 lbs. small potatoes
2 ½ cups water
Salt and pepper
Fat for frying

Fry chopped bacon, sausages and onions in the fat until onions are golden. Peel potatoes and add. Pour in water. Season, cover and simmer until potatoes are cooked.

12.   a) The Irish *crúb* means foot.

13.   c) Irish Stew

Irish Stew

Place mutton with thyme in saucepan and add stock to cover. Bring slowly to the boil and simmer for one hour. Add onions and potatoes, peeled and roughly chopped. Season. Continue cooking until vegetables are tender.

14.   All of these!

15.   a) Jonathan Swift

16.   d) Porter or stout is a dark brown beer made from roasted malt (Guinness is the most famous brand).

Porter Beef

2 tablespoons oil
2 bay leaves
2 lbs. rib steak, cut into large chunks
1 large onion, sliced
2 tablespoons seasoned flour
10 oz. Guinness
½ lb. mushrooms
10 oz. water or stock

Roll the meat in seasoned flour. Brown in hot fat and remove from pot. Add onion and fry gently for two-three minutes. Return meat to pot. Add other ingredients. Bring to the boil and simmer for two hours until meat is tender.

17.   a) Spiced beef

Spiced Beef

To be prepared two to three weeks before Christmas.

10–14 lbs. corned beef
½ oz. saltpeter
1 lb. salt
½ lb. brown suger
¼ lb. ground allspice

Rub sugar well into beef and leave for twelve hours. Rub in salt. Leave for twelve hours. Continue rubbing salt and sugar in daily for two to three weeks. Cover beef with cold water, bring to the boil, cover and simmer, allowing thirty minutes per pound, plus thirty minutes.

18.　d)　A traditional dish made with potatoes

Boxty on the griddle
Boxty on the pan
If you don't eat boxty
You'll never get a man!

An old Irish saying

Boxty

½ lb. raw potato
½ lb. mashed cooked potato
½ lb. plain flour
A little milk
1 egg
Salt and pepper

Grate raw potatoes and mix with mashed potato. Add salt, pepper and flour. Beat eggs and add to mixture with enough milk to make a dropping batter. Drop by tablespoonfuls onto a hot griddle or frying pan. Cook over a moderate heat for three to four minutes on each side.

19.　d)　Stomach lining

20.　a)　Cork

21.　b)　Kidneys

22.　a) and b) The drink and the evening meal

How to make an Irish pot of tea

Bring freshly drawn water to the boil in a kettle. Use a little to warm an earthenware teapot. Empty the pot, then add three to four teaspoons of good tea. Reboil the kettle.

Pour the water into the pot, then stir once. Cover the teapot with a cosy and let it brew for five minutes. Serve with milk and sugar.

23. a) Pancakes

24. a) Shrove Tuesday. Pancakes were traditionally eaten in order to use the surplus eggs, milk and butter before fasting began.

25. c) Brown Soda Bread

Brown Soda Bread

Sift together the dry ingredients. Mix the milk and egg and stir in. Mix, then knead on a floured surface until smooth. Shape into a round cake and place on a greased sheet, or into a greased loaf tin. Make a deep cross on the cake and bake in a hot oven at 375 degrees F for thirty-five to forty minutes. Brush with glaze (optional).

The mark of the cross is said to be the Sign of the Cross, made to bring the blessing of the Trinity on the bread so that none would be wasted.

26. c) Irish coffee

27. Try all four and decide.

28. b) A blood pudding

29. a) Cork

30. b) Punch, or hot whiskey

Punch

1 large measure Irish whiskey

1 teaspoon sugar
½ slice of orange
½ slice of lemon
6–8 cloves

Stud orange and lemon slices with cloves. Heat tumbler, add sugar, orange and lemon. Stir in whiskey and boiling water.

31. a) Toffee

32. b) An edible seaweed

33. b) Barm brack; in Irish *bairín breac* means a cake specked with fruit.

34. d) Scones

35. c) The Spanish

36. a) A young child, as presented in Swift's satire, "A Modest Proposal"

37. a) Sir Walter Raleigh

38. b) A type of Norway lobster

39. c) Goose

40. d) Brandy butter

Quotes

"The Irish are not in a conspiracy to cheat the world by false representations of the merits of their countrymen. No, sir; the Irish are a fair people; they never speak well of one another."

Dr. Samuel Johnson

1.   What American novelist said: "Give an Irishman lager for a month, and he's a dead man. An Irishman is lined with copper, and the beer corrodes it. But whiskey polishes the copper and is the saving of him"?
     a) Henry James
     b) Brendan Behan
     c) Mark Twain
     d) F. Scott Fitzgerald

2.   In an address to the Friendly Sons of St. Patrick in New York City on March 17, 1964, who said: "There is no doubt in my mind that nothing could have been started until the Irish invented politics"?
     a) Thomas P. O'Neill
     b) Robert Kennedy
     c) Jacob Javits
     d) Lyndon B. Johnson

3.   Who penned the following verse, from Ballad of the White Horse: "For the Great Gaels of Ireland/Are the men that God made mad,/For all their wars are merry/And all their songs are sad"?
a) W. B. Yeats
b) G. K. Chesterton
c) Robert Frost
d) Rudyard Kipling

4.   What British prime minister described Ireland in 1843 as "the bane of England and the opprobrium of Europe"?
a) William Gladstone
b) William Pitt
c) Benjamin Disraeli
d) Lloyd George

5.   What famous Irish actress said: "We're pragmatic. We say to the English and the Americans, 'All right, if you're fools enough to believe all this nonsense about us, go to it'"?
a) Angelica Huston
b) Maud Gonne
c) Siobhan McKenna
d) Kathleen ni Houlihan

6.   Who named Ireland "John Bull's Other Island"?
a) John Millington Synge
b) Oscar Wilde
c) George Bernard Shaw
d) John Bull

7.   What Irish novelist wrote in 1911: "My one claim to originality among Irishmen is that I never made a speech"?
a) James Joyce
b) Frank O'Connor
c) Maria Edgeworth
d) George Moore

8.   What famous Dubliner wrote: "The English and Americans dislike only some Irish—the same Irish that the Irish themselves detest, Irish writers—the ones that think"?
        a) Flann O'Brien
        b) Oliver St. John Gogarty
        c) Brendan Behan
        d) Danny Boyle

9.   Who wrote the following dialogue: "Pat: He was an Anglo-Irishman. Meg: In the blessed name of God, what's that? Pat: A Protestant with a horse."
        a) W. B. Yeats
        b) William Kennedy
        c) Eugene O'Neill
        d) Brendan Behan

10.   What famous American humorist said: "The English should give Ireland home rule—and reserve the motion picture rights"?
        a) Will Rogers
        b) Art Buchwald
        c) Mark Twain
        d) Finley Peter Dunne

11.   Who declared, "Other people have a nationality. The Irish and the Jews have a psychosis"?
        a) John F. Kennedy
        b) Woody Allen
        c) Brendan Behan
        d) Oscar Wilde

12.   What English satirist wrote the following dialogue between a young aristocrat and his butler: "You disapprove of the Swedes? Yes, Sir. Why? Their heads are too square, sir. And you disapprove of the Irish? Yes, Sir. Why? Because they are Irish, Sir."

a) Graham Greene
b) Tom Sharpe
c) P. G. Wodehouse
d) Kingsley Amis

13. What famous novelist penned the following verse: "This lovely land that has always sent/Her writers and artists to banishment/And in a spirit of Irish fun/Betrayed her own leaders, one by one.../Oh Ireland my first and only love/Where Christ and Caesar are hand in glove!/O lovely land where the shamrock grows!/(Allow me, ladies, to blow my nose)"?
    a) John O'Hara
    b) Brendan Behan
    c) Brian Moore
    d) James Joyce

14. What Irish dramatist said, in his description of the Aran Islands, "There is no language like the Irish for soothing and quieting"?
    a) Brian Friel
    b) Hugh Leonard
    c) John Millington Synge
    d) W. B. Yeats

15. Who defined Ireland as "the old sow that eats her farrow"?
    a) An anonymous twelfth-century writer
    b) Flann O'Brien
    c) Stephen Dedalus
    d) James Joyce

16. What nineteenth-century Irish immigrant declared, "Ireland is a fruitful mother of genius, but a barren nurse"?
    a) Eugene O'Neill
    b) Andrew Jackson
    c) James Hoban

d) John Boyle O'Reilly

17. What British writer wrote, "For where there are Irish there's loving and fighting/And when we stop either, it's Ireland no more"?
   a) G. K. Chesterton
   b) Rudyard Kipling
   c) E. M. Forster
   d) Isak Dinesen

18. Who said, "The Celt is thus peculiarly disposed to feel the spell of the feminine idiosyncrasy; he has an affinity to it; he is not far from its secret"?
   a) James Fenimore Cooper
   b) Matthew Arnold
   c) Charles Darwin
   d) Eugene O'Neill

19. What famous dramatist wrote, "An Irishman's heart is nothing but his imagination"?
   a) Tennesse Williams
   b) Eugene O'Neill
   c) George Bernard Shaw
   d) T. S. Eliot

20. What American poet wrote, "The Irish have the thickest ankles in the world/and the best complexions"?
   a) John Berryman
   b) Sylvia Plath
   c) E. E. Cummings
   d) Marianne Moore

21. What Irishwoman wrote, "The Irish have got gab but are too touchy to be humorous. Me too"?
   a) Kate O'Brien
   b) Lady Gregory

c) Mary Lavin
d) Edna O'Brien

22. What Irish short story writer said, "God made the grass, the air and the rain; and the grass, the air and the rain made the Irish; and the Irish turned the grass, the air and the rain back into God"?
   a) Frank O'Connor
   b) Mary Lavin
   c) Sean O'Faolain
   d) George Moore

23. What English dramatist wrote, "The Irish behave exactly as they have been protrayed as behaving for years. Charming, soft-voiced, quarrelsome, priest-ridden, feckless and happily devoid of the slightest integrity in our stodgy English sense of the word"?
   a) William Shakespeare
   b) Noel Coward
   c) William Congreve
   d) Tom Stoppard

24. What Irish-born dramatist said, "England had conquered Ireland, so there was nothing for it but to come over and conquer England, which you will notice I have done pretty thoroughly; one way or the other, my dear, we Irish will prevail"?
   a) Samuel Beckett
   b) George Bernard Shaw
   c) Brendan Behan
   d) Noel Coward

25. What Irish diplomat wrote in 1959, "Irishness is not primarily a question of birth or blood or language; it is the condition of being involved in the Irish situation, and usually of being mauled by it"?

a) Sean MacBride
b) Conor Cruise O'Brien
c) Lord Killanin
d) John F. Kennedy

26. What Irish poet wrote: "Out of Ireland have we come/Great hatred, little room/Maimed us at the start./I carry from my mother's womb/A fanatic's heart"?
a) Brian Merriman
b) Sean O Riordain
c) Seamus Heaney
d) William Butler Yeats

27. Who wrote, "Now Ireland has her madness and her weather still/For poetry makes nothing happen"?
a) Wallace Stevens
b) W. H. Auden
c) W. B. Yeats
d) Patrick Kavanagh

28. What American poet ends the poem "Spenser's Ireland" with the words: "I am troubled, I'm dissatisfied, I'm Irish"?
a) Galway Kinnell
b) Marianne Moore
c) Wallace Stevens
d) John Berryman

29. To what New York mayor did Franklin D. Roosevelt address the following question: "Why do you Irish always answer a question with a question"?
a) John Lindsay
b) Jimmy Walker
c) Fiorello La Guardia
d) Al Smith

30. What was his reply?
    a) "What gave you that idea?"
    b) "Mind your own business."
    c) "Do we now?"
    d) "I dunno."

31. What governor of New York said, on March 14, 1975, "There's no such thing as a merry Irish song"?
    a) Hugh Carey
    b) Al Smith
    c) Mario Cuomo
    d) James Roosevelt

32. Who said in the *New York Times* in 1971, "The actual Irish weather report is really a recording made in 1922, which no one has had occasion to change. 'Scattered showers, periods of sunshine'"?
    a) Wilfrid Sheed
    b) Leon Uris
    c) Edward Kennedy
    d) Daniel Moynihan

33. Who wrote, "English, Scotchmen, Jews, do well in Ireland—Irishmen never; even the patriot has to leave Ireland to get a hearing"?
    a) James Joyce
    b) John McGahern
    c) George Moore
    d) Samuel Beckett

34. Who said of his seventeenth-century invasion, "It has pleased God to bless our endeavours at Drogheda"?
    a) William of Orange
    b) Oliver Cromwell
    c) Wolfe Tone
    d) Eoin Rua O'Neill

35. Who wrote, "Dublin, though a place much worse than London, is not as bad as Iceland"?
    a) Samuel Johnson
    b) Oliver Goldsmith
    c) W. H. Auden
    d) Joseph Conrad

36. What nineteenth-century Irish leader said, "The hospitality of an Irishman is not the running account of posted and ledgered courtesies, as in other countries; it springs, like all his qualities, his faults, his virtues, directly from his heart"?
    a) Charles Stewart Parnell
    b) Daniel O'Connell
    c) Wolfe Tone
    d) Robert Emmet

37. Who wrote, within two hours of landing in Ireland, "I had no conception the stories of Ireland were so true. I had fancied all were violent exaggeration. But it is impossible to exaggerate"?
    a) Pope John Paul II
    b) John Ruskin
    c) John F. Kennedy
    d) Charles Darwin

38. Who wrote, during her visit to Ireland, "It is a lovely country, but very melancholy, except that people never stop talking"?
    a) Queen Victoria
    b) Marianne Moore
    c) Virginia Woolf
    d) Iris Murdoch

39. Who said, "Your first day in Dublin is always your worst"?
    a) John Berryman

b) Jonathan Swift
c) W. B. Yeats
d) Seamus Heaney

40. Who said, "I would have liked to go to Ireland but my grandmother would not let me. Perhaps she thought I wanted to take the little place"?
a) Henry II
b) James II
c) Kaiser Wilhelm II
d) Theodore Roosevelt

41. Who was his grandmother?
a) Queen Elizabeth
b) Queen Victoria
c) Mary Stuart
d) Princess Anne of Denmark

42. What American writer, visiting Ireland in 1895, wrote, "I was deeply moved by the tragic shabbiness of this sinister country"?
a) Mark Twain
b) Henry James
c) Harriet Beecher Stowe
d) F. Scott Fitzgerald

43. Who recalled a first visit to Ireland in the following way: "I saw a fleet of fishing boats...I flew down, almost touching the craft, and yelled at them, asking if I was on the right road to Ireland. They just stared. Maybe they didn't hear me. Maybe I didn't hear them. Or maybe they thought I was just a crazy fool. An hour later I saw land"?
a) Amelia Earhart
b) William Alcock
c) Charles Lindbergh
d) Lyndon Johnson

44. Who said, "If you ever come to America, come to Washington and tell them, at the gate, that you come from Galway. The word will be out—it will be *Céad Míle Fáilte*"?
    a) Ronald Reagan
    b) Richard Nixon
    c) Jimmy Carter
    d) John F. Kennedy

45. What English satirist said, "You can't get into the soup in Ireland, do what you like"?
    a) P. G. Wodehouse
    b) Noel Coward
    c) Evelyn Waugh
    d) Graham Greene

46. Who declared, in an address to the Irish Parliament on June 4, 1984, "I can perhaps claim to be an Irishman longer than anyone here"?
    a) Margaret Thatcher
    b) Thomas P. O'Neill
    c) Ronald Reagan
    d) Juan Carlos

47. Who said, "It takes both courage and patience to live in Ireland"?
    a) John Huston
    b) James Joyce
    c) Sean O'Casey
    d) John F. Kennedy

48. Who said: "Americans adore me and will go on adoring me until I say something nice about them"?
    a) Oscar Wilde
    b) George Bernard Shaw
    c) Bono
    d) Bob Geldof

49. Who declared, "We have really everything in common with America nowadays, except, of course, language"?
    a) Oscar Wilde
    b) Oliver St. John Gogarty
    c) Lady Gregory
    d) Jonathan Swift

50. What did Oscar Wilde describe as "simply a vast unnecessary amount of water going the wrong way"?
    a) The Mississippi River
    b) The Thames
    c) Niagara Falls
    d) The Shannon River

51. Who said, "The youth of America is their oldest tradition, it has been going on now for three hundred years"?
    a) G. B. Shaw
    b) John Bull
    c) John Boyle O'Reilly
    d) Oscar Wilde

52. Of what American politician did the *Irish Independent* say, "After three generations, a young man of fully Irish stock has reached the last point of integration into American life — the chief executive post of the nation"?
    a) Ronald Reagan
    b) John F. Kennedy
    c) Andrew Johnson
    d) James Garfield

Answers

1.   c)   Mark Twain in *Life on the Mississippi*

2.   d)   Lyndon B. Johnson

3.   b)   G. K. Chesterton

4.   c)   Disraeli

5.   c)   Siobhan McKenna

6.   c)   G. B. Shaw

7.   d)   George Moore

8.   c)   Brendan Behan

9.   d)   Brendan Behan, in *The Hostage*

10.   a) Will Rogers, in *The Autobiography of Will Rogers*

11.   c) Oscar Wilde

12.   a) Graham Greene

13.   d) Joyce, in his poem "Gas from a Burner"

14.   c) J. M. Synge

15.   c) and d) Stephen Dedalus in James Joyce's *Portrait of the Artist as a Young Man*

16.   d) John Boyle O'Reilly

17.   b) Rudyard Kipling

18.   b) Matthew Arnold, in *On the Study of Celtic Literature*

19.   c) G. B. Shaw, in *John Bull's Other Island*

20.   a) John Berryman, *The Dream Songs*

21.   d) Edna O'Brien

22.   c) Sean O'Faolain

23.   b) Noel Coward

24.   b) G. B. Shaw

25.   b) Conor Cruise O'Brien

26.   d) W. B. Yeats

27.   b) W. H. Auden

28. b) Marianne Moore

29. b) Jimmy Walker

30. c) Do we now?

31. a) Hugh Carey

32. a) Wilfrid Sheed

33. c) George Moore, in *Ave* in 1911

34. b) Oliver Cromwell

35. a) Samuel Johnson

36. b) Daniel O'Connell

37. b) John Ruskin

38. c) Virginia Woolf

39. a) John Berryman, in *Dream Songs*

40. c) Kaiser Wilhelm II of Germany

41. b) Queen Victoria

42. b) Henry James

43. c) Charles Lindbergh

44. d) John F. Kennedy

45. c) Evelyn Waugh, in *Decline and Fall*

46.   c) Ronald Reagan

47.   c) Sean O'Casey

48.   b) G. B. Shaw

49.   a) Oscar Wilde

50.   c) Niagara Falls

51.   d) Oscar Wilde

52.   b) John F. Kennedy